Reading Comprehension

in Varied Subject Matter

JANE ERVIN

SOCIAL STUDIES

LITERATURE   MATHEMATICS

SCIENCE   THE ARTS

PHILOSOPHY, LOGIC, AND LANGUAGE

COMBINED SUBJECTS

EDUCATORS PUBLISHING SERVICE
Cambridge and Toronto

Dr. Jane Ervin works in Washington, D.C. with children with reading and learning problems and advises parents on educational needs. Her advice is sought by schools, government, and educational and parent organizations throughout the country. Dr. Ervin has been principal of a school, taught children of all ages, and trained teachers in reading and basic skills. She received her doctorate in education and post-doctorate diploma in English from UCLA.

ACKNOWLEDGMENTS

Dr. Ervin would like to thank the following subject specialists, who collaborated with her in developing these books:

Mary N. Allen — mathematics and social studies

Kazuko Furuya — elementary grades

Judith D. Jones — science

Margot Rapersby — English and the arts

Margaret Fife Tanguay — English

Dr. Ervin would particularly like to thank the National Geographic Society editorial staff for their interest in the development of these books. The inclusion of excerpts from National Geographic books and the School Bulletin in both adapted and reprinted form has contributed greatly to the quality of these books.

Printed in USA

ISBN 978-0-8388-0600-5

9 10 11 12 MNG 11 10 09

TO THE STUDENT

Each selection in this workbook is on a theme that reappears in each book in the series. For example, Selection 5 in each book is about "The Story of America"; Selection 12 asks "What is the Biggest?" while Selection 26 is on "Rhythm, Repetition, and Sound."

Each book also has themes, or topics, that relate the selections within the book to one another, show different aspects of a topic, and help you to gain a broader knowledge of a subject. The themes in Book 1 are as follows: Origins and Creation; Small and Big; Eggs; Woodpeckers; and Maps. Look for these topics, and how they are treated, as you read the selections.

CONTENTS

subject: combined subjects

subject: social studies

subject: science

subject: philosophy, logic, and language

Selection 1 (Sample)*—Subject: Combined Subjects
Theme: The World of Then and Now

THE BEGINNING OF THE WORLD

ABOUT THE PASSAGE   Almost as long as people have existed they have told stories about how the earth was first made. This is one story. As you read, use your imagination. Try to see the earth being formed just as the space family on Mars is seeing it.

REASON FOR READING   To use your imagination as you read.

READ THE PASSAGE

''There are never any good programs on these days,'' Mrs. Martian says, as she turns from one channel to another on her big color TV.

"Wait, what was that on the outer-space channel?" her husband asks. "I heard the woman say this was the most exciting thing to happen for years. What do you think it is?"

Mrs. Martian quickly turns to the channel, and the couple hears the following report:

"Yes, **residents** of Mars, this is the most exciting **event** you will ever see—well, at least for a while. We are seeing, through our **latest telescopes,** the beginning of another world.

"Watch how the large ball of fire is changing. It is **cooling** and its outside is becoming hard and rock-like.

Now there's a storm. It's raining heavily. Look at those **streaks** of lightning! They should be beautiful on your astro-color TV screen.

"The storm is over, but look at all those oceans and lakes it has left behind. I can see all sorts of shapes moving in the water. Some of them are crawling onto the land, which has so many nice green plants growing on it. My goodness, the place is full of animals, insects, and reptiles. And look, some of these seem to be changing form! I do believe I see a human being. Oh, dear! That **probably** means we'll be having visitors some day."

Mrs. Martian switches off the TV. "My, that was quite a long program. Do you know, it took over five billion years? I think it's time for bed."

*For this sample selection, answer the questions that have no answers given.

THINKING IT OVER

(1) About how long did it take to create the world? *It took about five billion years.*

(2) What did the TV announcer think when she saw human beings? *She thought the residents of Mars would have visitors some day.*

(3) What did she mean by "have some visitors some day"? _____

_____

STUDYING THE PASSAGE

(1) Find the Main Idea: Choose one.
    (a) Life on Mars.
    (b) Watching a long TV program.
    (c) How the world began.
    (d) How human beings were created.   *c*

(2) Find the Facts: Mark each one *true* or *false*.
    (a) The people watching the creation of the world were living on a planet in outer space.   (a) *T*
    (b) The world's surface became hard as it cooled.   (b) *T*
    (c) Oceans and lakes suddenly appeared from nowhere.   (c) *F*
    (d) Animal life first came from the sea.   (d) ____
    (e) Life first came out of the mountains.   (e) ____
    (f) The trees and plants made the earth green.   (f) ____

(3) Find the Order: Number the following in the order in which they appear in the passage.
    (a) The rains came.   *3*
    (b) Human beings appeared.   *5*
    (c) The world cooled.   ____
    (d) The world was a ball of whirling fire.   ____
    (e) Plants, animals, and insects appeared.   ____

(4) Go beyond the Facts: How does the writer tell you about the beginning of the world? Choose one answer.
   (a) By imagining how it will happen in the future.
   (b) By explaining how it happened in the past.
   (c) By pretending it is happening now.
   (d) By telling us several different ways the world began. _____

USING THE WORDS

(1) Words and Their Meanings: Write the letter of the correct definition beside the word. One word has *two* meanings.

   _h_ resident   (a) most recent
   _d_ event   (b) losing heat
   _a_ latest   (c) fit or spell ("a talking _____")
   ____ telescope   (d) unusual happening, occasion
   ____ cooling   (e) bolt
   ____ streak   (f) very likely
                         (g) instrument that makes far away objects look closer
   ____ probably   and bigger than they are
                         (h) person who lives in a certain place

(2) Write a paragraph using 2 of the vocabulary words. Use a separate piece of paper.

WRITING ABOUT IT   Use a separate piece of paper for your answers.

(1) The writer uses people talking to one another to tell the story. This is called "dialogue." Write your own story using dialogue.

(2) The Martians are watching the world on television. Imagine you see another planet on television. Write about what you see there.

HOW INSECTS COMMUNICATE

ABOUT THE PASSAGE

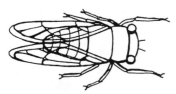

Human beings talk to each other, but they cannot talk to insects. However, insects can **communicate** with each other, and there are several ways that they do this.

REASON FOR READING

To learn what ways insects use to talk to each other.

READ THE PASSAGE

Have you ever tried to tell people something by buzzing at them? Or have you and a friend ever had a nice chat by **scratching** your bodies? No? Well, you would have if you were an insect, for this is how insects "talk" to one another.

Human beings use a **variety** of ways to talk to one another. As well as **producing** sounds from their mouths, they use their faces, hands and arms to communicate. For example, they smile when they are happy and point with a finger to show which way to go. Insects, however, usually use only one way to communicate.

The buzzing noise of bees and wasps comes from the tiny air pipes in different parts of their bodies. The air **rushing** through these pipes makes them **vibrate,** thus producing the noise we hear.

The cicada (si-kay-duh), a large fly-like insect, is probably the noisiest "talker" of all the insects. The skin on its stomach acts like the skin of a drum. It beats this "drum" by moving its stomach muscles. These muscle movements make the drum tighten and then loosen, producing the noise you hear.

Another noisy talker is the katydid, a kind of grasshopper. It **scrapes** its front wings and legs together as if it were playing the violin. This makes a noise like a creaky door. The katydid's ears are on its forelegs instead of on its head.

Each insect knows only one tune. It is the tune that has been played by all the insects of its kind for millions of years. Thus it is easy for all the insects of one family to find each other. Sometimes the noise **scares** away their enemies.

THINKING IT OVER

(1) Can insects "talk" to one another? _____

_____

(2) Which insect has ears on its forelegs? _____

_____

(3) How many tunes can insects play? _____

_____

STUDYING THE PASSAGE

(1) Find the Main Idea: Choose one.
    (a) How noisy insects are.
    (b) How insects communicate.
    (c) How insects frighten their enemies.
    (d) How humans use their voices to talk with one another.   _____

(2) Find the Facts: Mark each one *true* or *false*.
    (a) Humans use only their breath to communicate.   (a) _____
    (b) Bees and wasps make a buzzing noise by rubbing their wings
        together.   (b) _____
    (c) The cicada (large flying insect) could be called the
        "Insect Drummer."   (c) _____
    (d) The katydid (like a grasshopper) makes a noise by scraping
        its front wings and legs together.   (d) _____
    (e) Each insect knows only one tune.   (e) _____
    (f) Insects use noise to let other insects in their family know
        where they are.   (f) _____

(3) Find the Order: Number the following in the order in which they appear in the passage.

(a) Bees and wasps make a buzzing sound.

(b) Insects use different parts of their bodies to communicate. _____

(c) The cicada is probably the noisiest "talker" of all insects. _____

(d) Today insects make the same noises as they did millions of years ago.

(e) The katydid makes a noise like a creaky door. _____

(4) Go beyond the Facts. Choose one.

(a) Insects cannot talk and hear.

(b) Insects can talk and hear like human beings.

(c) Insects can talk and hear, but not like human beings.

(d) All insects talk and hear the same way. _____

USING THE WORDS

(1) Words and Their Meanings: Write the letter of the correct definition beside the word. One word has *two* meanings.

_____ to communicate	(a)	to give and receive information
_____ to scratch	(b)	hurrying, going in suddenly with force
_____	(c)	to rub gently to stop an itch
_____ variety	(d)	to rub to make a tiny sound
_____ to produce	(e)	to rub roughly and noisily
_____ rushing	(f)	to move quickly back and forth
_____ to vibrate	(g)	to frighten
_____ to scrape	(h)	different kinds
_____ to scare	(i)	to make

(2) Write a paragraph using 2 of the vocabulary words. Use a separate piece of paper.

WRITING ABOUT IT   Use a separate piece of paper for your answers.

(1) Write a paragraph explaining why you cannot talk to an insect.

(2) Practice writing dialogue. Imagine you could talk to an insect. Describe your conversation.

6

GETTING AROUND

ABOUT THE PASSAGE

People have always moved from place to place on the earth, but the ways they have moved themselves and their belongings have changed many times.

REASON FOR READING

As you read this passage, notice how the writer organizes her information. How does she tell you about the different methods of transportation?

(a) She talks about transportation in different countries.

(b) She tells us how methods of transportation have changed over the years.

(c) She tells a story.

(d) She compares the best and worst things about different ways of traveling.

READ THE PASSAGE

"O.K., let's go!" How many times this must have been said over the years! But how many different ways men, women, and children have traveled from one place to another!

People first traveled (and of course still do) on their own two feet. Later, people **tamed** animals and rode them. They used many different kinds of animals, such as oxen, camels, and elephants. The animals people rode most often, however, belonged to the horse family, which includes horses, donkeys, and mules.

Next, men and women built wagons that they **attached** to the animals, so more people could travel at one time. This was a big "step" forward. Why? Because it was the first time people used a wheel.

The **discovery** of the wheel made traveling much easier. The first wheel was not very well made, but over the years it has been improved. Today our automobiles move along the highways with speed and **comfort.**

Another way men and women have traveled has been on water. Early people made rivers their highways by floating down them on boats made from trees. Soon oars and sails were developed. These enabled the boats to go against the flow of the rivers. Later, as people became more clever, they **invented en-**

7

gines, which made sailing against the river much easier. They also used these engines on land, and after that to fly into the air. Now men and women have made rockets to explore a new world—outer space.

THINKING IT OVER

(1) Give three methods of transportation that the writer talks about. _____

_____

(2) What were the *two* most important discoveries that made transportation easier,

faster, and more comfortable? _____

_____

STUDYING THE PASSAGE

(1) Find the Main Idea: Choose one.
  (a) Animals are used in transportation.
  (b) Wheels made traveling much easier.
  (c) Transportation has improved through the ages.
  (d) Space travel is the latest thing.   _____

(2) Find the Facts: Mark each one *true* or *false*.
  (a) The first form of travel was walking.   (a) ____
  (b) People tamed animals to improve transportation.   (b) ____
  (c) Camels are the most frequently used transport animal. (c) ____
  (d) The wheel was a very significant discovery.   (d) ____
  (e) Sailboats were first used on canals.   (e) ____
  (f) The invention of engines improved transportation.   (f) ____

(3) Find the Order: Number the following in the order in which they appear in the passage.
  (a) People invented the wheel.   _____
  (b) People invented engines to be able to move faster.   _____
  (c) People walked.   _____
  (d) People learned to fly into the air.   _____
  (e) People tamed animals to aid transportation.   _____

(4) Go beyond the Facts: How does the writer tell us about different means of transportation? Choose one answer.

   (a) She talks about transportation in different countries.

   (b) She tells us how methods of transportation have changed over the years.

   (c) She tells a story.

   (d) She compares the best and worst things about different ways of traveling.   _____

USING THE WORDS

(1) Words and Their Meanings: Write the letter of the correct definition beside the word. One word has *two* meanings.

   _____ to tame   (a) ease and well-being
   _____ to attach   (b) to connect
   _____ discovery   (c) a machine that uses energy, in this case to move something
   _____ comfort   (d) to create or figure out; to produce for the first time
   _____   (e) to make someone feel better
   _____ to invent   (f) to make a wild animal gentle
   _____ engine   (g) knowledge of something for the first time

(2) Write a paragraph using 2 of the vocabulary words. Use a separate piece of paper.

WRITING ABOUT IT   Use a separate piece of paper for your answers.

(1) Think about the discovery of the wheel. Tell about the different ways it has helped us move from one place to another.

(2) Describe your favorite method of transportation and why you like it. It can be a regular way, such as a bus or a bike. Or it can be a fun way, such as a skateboard or sled.

Selection 4—Subject: Social Studies
Theme: What America Means—Traditions and Symbols

THE STARS AND STRIPES*

ABOUT THE PASSAGE

Americans show their patriotism by pledging **allegiance** to the flag. The American flag is a **symbol**—that is, it stands for more than the cloth from which it is made. But lots of people do not know how the flag got these other meanings.

REASON FOR READING

To learn what the flag means and how it got these meanings.

READ THE PASSAGE

"I pledge allegiance to the flag of the United States of America, and to the Republic for which it stands, one Nation under God, **indivisible,** with **liberty** and **justice** for all."

When people stand **at attention** and say this pledge, they are showing their patriotism, love, and respect for America. Our flag, the Stars and Stripes, is a symbol. It stands for the United States of America.

Each of the fifty stars stands for one state, and the thirteen red and white stripes stand for the original thirteen states in our country. Each color in the flag has a meaning. Red stands for bravery or **valor.** White stands for purity, and blue stands for justice or fairness.

The people who helped our nation in its earliest days chose these colors and these ideas to express the kind of country they hoped ours would be. And today, as then, our nation and its people believe that we must be brave, stand for what is right, and have fair and just laws for every citizen.

The American flag was designed by a man named Francis Hopkinson. For a long time, however, people believed that Betsy Ross made the first flag. Now it is believed that this is a legend begun by her family. Our flag was officially **adopted** by the Continental Congress in 1777.

---

*Adapted from *Our Flag: The Stars and Stripes*, by Elizabeth Russell Plaisted.

THINKING IT OVER

(1) What do the colors in the American flag stand for?

    (a) red _____

    (b) white_____

    (c) blue _____

(2) Explain what "patriotism" means: _____
_____

(3) Who designed the flag? _____
_____

STUDYING THE PASSAGE

(1) Find the Main Idea: Choose one.
    (a) Why we say the pledge of allegiance.
    (b) The meaning of our flag.
    (c) Where our flag came from.
    (d) Why our flag is colored. _____

(2) Find the Facts: Mark each one *true* or *false*.
    (a) By saying the pledge of allegiance to the flag, we show our loyalty to the United States.   (a) ____
    (b) The colors of the flag were chosen to be the same as the flag of England because the Pilgrims came from there.   (b) ____
    (c) Each color of the flag has a special meaning.   (c) ____
    (d) Americans believe there should be different laws for different groups of people.   (d) ____
    (e) For many years people thought the first flag was made by Betsy Ross.   (e) ____
    (f) The flag was officially adopted in 1777.   (f) ____

(3) Find the Order: Number the following in the order in which they appear in the passage.

   (a) The flag was adopted by the Continental Congress. ____

   (b) The people who helped our nation in its earliest days chose its colors. ____

   (c) Our flag stands for the United States of America. ____

   (d) People pledge allegiance to the flag and the republic for which it stands. ____

   (e) Today, as then, our people believe we must stand for what is right and fair. ____

(4) Go beyond the Facts: Which *one* can you conclude from the passage?

   (a) The flag must have been expensive to make.

   (b) Our flag stands for different things today than in the days of the early settlers.

   (c) Americans still believe in some of the same things that the early settlers believed in.

   (d) People have less respect for the flag today. ____

USING THE WORDS

(1) Words and Their Meanings: Write the letter of the correct definition beside the word. One word has *two* meanings.

   ____ allegiance   (a) erect, motionless position

   ____ symbol   (b) courage, fearlessness

   ____ indivisible   (c) to vote in (a resolution or agreement)

   ____ liberty   (d) loyalty to one's country

   ____ justice   (e) to accept; to take under protection

   ____ valor   (f) fairness

   ____ to adopt   (g) undivided, one

   ____   (h) something that stands for something else

   ____ at attention   (i) freedom

(2) Write a paragraph using 2 of the vocabulary words. Use a separate piece of paper.

WRITING ABOUT IT   Use a separate piece of paper for your answers.

(1) Make up a speech explaining why you love and respect your country.

(2) If you could choose a symbol for America, what would it be? Describe your symbol, and explain why you chose it.

SACAJAWEA

ABOUT THE PASSAGE

A river, a mountain pass, and a peak have been named after this woman. Monuments and statues have been raised in her honor. Her name is Sacajawea. Who was she?

REASON FOR READING

To find out what Sacajawea did to get such attention.

READ THE PASSAGE

Sacajawea listened as her husband told her the exciting news. Lewis and Clark had agreed to take him on their trip across the unknown country to the West Coast.

"I'm going with you," Sacajawea told him.

"You can't," replied her husband. "It'll be dangerous. Besides Lewis and Clark don't want a seventeen-year-old with a child tagging along."

"I won't tag along. I'll be very useful," said Sacajawea. And, that day, she persuaded Lewis and Clark to take her and her child.

In 1805 they set out with the group of forty men. They paddled their canoes up the Missouri River. Sometimes it was very hot, sometimes cold and damp. They trudged along the shore, stumbling over rocks, through brush, and up steep slopes. They met bears, unknown people, and sickness.

Sacajawea kept up, her child strapped to her back. She had a good **sense of direction** and helped find trails through the forests and over the mountains. She also showed the men wild plants and roots that they could eat when they were hungry. She even cured their ills through her knowledge of **herbs.**

More than once Sacajawea saved the expedition. When a sudden gust of wind overturned the group's canoe, she dived into the water and rescued **vital** supplies, records, and instruments. Later, when they met her relatives, the Shoshone, she **persuaded** them to give the group guides and horses to cross the Rocky Mountains.

They traveled across the mountains, down the Columbia River, and over the unknown land until they finally made it to the West Coast and the Pacific Ocean.

Then they had to face the return trip. It was just as difficult. Once again the **courageous** group succeeded, and

14

once again Sacajawea proved to be **loyal,** useful, and brave.

The Lewis and Clark expedition was an important part of United States history. Its success brought knowledge about newly **acquired,** unknown **territory.** This success owes much to Sacajawea.

THINKING IT OVER

(1) How did Sacajawea help to make the expedition successful?_____

_____

(2) Which of the following do you think Sacajawea was?
    (a) A Native American.
    (b) A Pacific Islander.
    (c) An African American.
    (d) A European.   _____

STUDYING THE PASSAGE

(1) Find the Main Idea: Choose one.
    (a) How Lewis and Clark crossed the country.
    (b) Exploring unknown lands.
    (c) How Sacajawea's people could not be depended upon.
    (d) How Sacajawea contributed to the expedition.   _____

(2) Find the Facts: Mark each one *true* or *false.*
    (a) The group set out in 1805.   (a) _____
    (b) Sacajawea's husband carried her baby.   (b) _____
    (c) Sacajawea was carried over the difficult mountain trails.   (c) _____
    (d) Sacajawea helped find trails across the mountains.   (d) _____
    (e) Sacajawea asked her relatives for help.   (e) _____
    (f) Sacajawea did not make the return trip with the group.   (f) _____

(3) Find the Order: Number the following in the order in which they appear in the passage.

(a) She dived into the water. _____

(b) They paddled their canoes up the Missouri River. _____

(c) She also showed the men wild plants and roots. _____

(d) The Lewis and Clark expedition was an important part of United States history. _____

(e) Sacajawea said she was going, too. _____

(4) Go beyond the Facts: Choose *one* reason why Sacajawea wanted to join the expedition.

(a) Lewis and Clark were eager to have her as a guide.

(b) She knew she would make history.

(c) She had never been west before.

(d) She was used to life in the wilderness and felt she could be useful. _____

USING THE WORDS

(1) Words and Their Meanings: Write the letter of the correct definition beside the word.

_____ sense of direction	(a) faithful
_____ herbs	(b) necessary
_____ vital	(c) brave
_____ persuaded	(d) obtained, got
_____ courageous	(e) land
_____ loyal	(f) ability to guess the way to go
_____ acquired	(g) convinced someone to do something
_____ territory	(h) plants used in medicine and cooking

(2) Write a paragraph using 2 of the vocabulary words. Use a separate piece of paper.

WRITING ABOUT IT   Use a separate piece of paper for your answers.

(1) Describe the difficulties Sacajawea and the others had to face on the trip.

(2) Would you have liked to have gone on the trip? Give reasons for your answer.

FROM A SMALL BEGINNING TO A GREAT POSITION

ABOUT THE PASSAGE

A poor, young boy growing up on the frontier during America's early years studied and worked hard. When he failed, he still kept trying. Finally he became the seventh president of the United States. His name was Andrew Jackson.

REASON FOR READING

To learn how hard one person worked to get what he wanted.

READ THE PASSAGE

America has often been called the land of **opportunity.** It is a place where a person can **achieve success** if he or she has the right capabilities and enough **determination.** President Andrew Jackson proved to us that in America poor children can dream of reaching the top.

Jackson was born in 1767 on the frontier of the Carolinas. He had little opportunity for much education. After the close of the American Revolution, Jackson studied law. He practiced law in an area that was to become the state of Tennessee. He was important in the formation of that state. Jackson became a U.S. **representative** from Tennessee at the young age of twenty-nine. He became a U.S. senator at thirty.

Jackson became a general in the Tennessee militia in 1802. He achieved great success and fame in the War of 1812. His victory at the battle of New Orleans made him the hero of many Americans.

Jackson's great success led to the suggestion that he enter the 1824 race for the presidency. In this race he met with a great **setback.** Although he won the greatest number of votes, he did not win a **majority.** The election was decided by the House of Representatives. John Quincy Adams was named president.

Most people would have given up, but Jackson continued to work hard. In 1828 he won the presidency. He proved that with **drive** and determination any American can reach the greatest **position** in the land.

THINKING IT OVER

(1) Andrew Jackson had one setback. What was it? _____

_____

(2) What was Andrew Jackson's first job?_____

_____

STUDYING THE PASSAGE

(1) Find the Main Idea: Choose one.
   (a) Jackson fought in the War of 1812.
   (b) Jackson was the youngest president.
   (c) A poor child can become famous in America.
   (d) You need money to reach the highest position in the United States. ____

(2) Find the Facts: Mark each one *true* or *false*.
   (a) Andrew Jackson's family came from a big city.   (a) ____
   (b) Andrew Jackson had a very good education.   (b) ____
   (c) Jackson became a lawyer.   (c) ____
   (d) Mr. Jackson was once a senator.   (d) ____
   (e) Jackson lost the election in 1824.   (e) ____
   (f) Andrew Jackson won the presidency in 1828.   (f) ____

(3) Find the Order: Number the following in the order in which they appear
   in the passage.
   (a) Any American can reach a great position in this land.   ____
   (b) He achieved great success in the War of 1812.   ____
   (c) In 1824, John Quincy Adams was named president.   ____
   (d) Jackson practiced law in the area that would one day become
       the state of Tennessee.   ____
   (e) In America poor children can dream of reaching the top.   ____

(4) Go beyond the Facts: This passage suggests which *two* of the following?

    (a) It is easier to do well if you are a boy, rather than a girl.

    (b) You should learn all you can while in school.

    (c) Losers should try again.

    (d) Hard work often helps you win something you try for.   ____ ____

USING THE WORDS

(1) Words and Their Meanings: Write the letter of the correct definition beside the word. One word has *two* meanings.

____ opportunity	(a)	winning something you try for
____ to achieve	(b)	chosen by the people
____ success	(c)	energy; force
____ determination	(d)	defeat coming after victories
____ representative	(e)	chance to do something
____ setback	(f)	a number greater than half of the total
____ majority	(g)	strong will to do something
____ drive	(h)	to make something move and to direct it
____	(i)	job; rank
____ position	(j)	to do well, to finish something with success

(2) Write a paragraph using 2 of the vocabulary words. Use a separate piece of paper.

WRITING ABOUT IT   Use a separate piece of paper for your answers.

(1) A time line shows events in the order in which they happened. Make a time line showing the important events in Andrew Jackson's life.

(2) Jackson had a big disappointment when he did not get elected. Describe a disappointment you have had.

Selection 7—Subject: Social Studies
Theme: How Others Live

SPRING CELEBRATIONS*

ABOUT THE PASSAGE

Spring is a time of **rebirth** and new hope. Throughout the ages people in many different countries have had special **celebrations** at this time of year.

REASON FOR READING

To find out about one of the many things people have in common and also to see how an egg can be used as a symbol (one thing which stands for something else).

READ THE PASSAGE

When the last snow melts and everything becomes green again, you probably feel very happy. You know that summer is coming, and you will be able to be outdoors in the sun. People all over the world for thousands of years have felt the same way; they have celebrated the coming of spring and the rebirth of nature. While **customs** differ from one place to another, many use eggs as a sign of new life.

To Christians, springtime is Easter time. Easter is a **religious** holiday celebrating the rebirth of Christ. Many Easter customs have to do with eggs: **decorating** them, hiding them, and eating them. Some of the most beautiful Easter eggs are Ukranian. These are decorated with small,

detailed designs that are amazing to examine. In the United States, children paint Easter eggs and play ''hunt the egg.''

For Jews, springtime is Passover time. Passover is a celebration of the Jews' **escape** from slavery to freedom. Since freedom after slavery is like a new life, Passover is also a celebration of new beginnings. People eat eggs during special holiday meals because for them eggs stand for freedom, new beginnings, and new life.

Many old European customs emphasize eggs as a symbol of rebirth and love. In Hungary, a boy **earns** a colored egg if he can splash a girl with **perfumed** water. In parts of Germany, girls go into the woods in the springtime and

*Adapted by permission of the publisher from *The Golden Bough: A Study in Magic and Religion*, by Sir James George Frazer. Copyright 1922 by The MacMillan Company.

bring back a tree decorated with green, red, and white ribbons. As they carry the colorful tree home, they sing

> "Spring comes to visit us,
>   With eggs that are red,
>   With yellow pancakes. . . .
> We are carrying Summer
>   into the village."

In northern England, rolling colored eggs down slopes on Easter Monday is popular, while rolling eggs across the White House lawn has become a tradition in the United States.

In ancient times Egyptians and Persians celebrated their spring festivals by coloring and eating eggs. They thought the world was actually created in the spring. Some of them thought that at first the world itself was one huge egg!

THINKING IT OVER

(1) Eggs are symbols of what things?

    (a) _____

    (b) _____

    (c) _____

STUDYING THE PASSAGE

(1) Find the Main Idea: Choose one.
    (a) Easter is a springtime celebration.
    (b) Eggs stand for new life all over the world.
    (c) The world was one huge egg.
    (d) Easter celebrates rebirth and new beginnings.   _____

(2) Find the Facts: Mark each one *true* or *false*.
    (a) Springtime is celebrated only in America.   (a) ____
    (b) Many Easter customs have to do with eggs.   (b) ____
    (c) Children hunt Easter rabbits.   (c) ____
    (d) German girls bring back a decorated tree.   (d) ____
    (e) In Hungary, the boy gets an egg if he can jump over a wooden barrier.   (e) ____
    (f) Passover is a celebration of freedom.   (f) ____

(3) Find the Order: Number the following in the order in which they appear in the passage.

    (a) Easter is a religious holiday celebrating the rebirth of Christ. _____

    (b) At first the world was one huge egg. _____

    (c) You will be able to go outdoors in the sun. _____

    (d) "We are carrying Summer into the village." _____

    (e) The Jews escaped from slavery into freedom. _____

(4) Go beyond the Facts: Choose one.

    (a) Easter eggs are not really Christian.

    (b) There must have been a huge chicken who laid the egg of the world.

    (c) Eggs are only for children.

    (d) Spring is very important to people all over the world. _____

USING THE WORDS

(1) Words and Their Meanings: Write the letter of the correct definition beside the word. The first word has *two* meanings.

_____ rebirth	(a)	a usual course of action, a habit
_____	(b)	to add ornaments and color
_____ to celebrate	(c)	to make a day or event special by doing things that are fun
_____ custom		
_____ religious	(d)	being born again
_____ to decorate	(e)	sweet-smelling
_____ to escape	(f)	to get away from or out of something bad
_____ to earn	(g)	becoming better, becoming like new
_____ perfumed	(h)	related to belief in God or gods
	(i)	to receive for working

(2) Write a paragraph using 2 of the vocabulary words. Use a separate piece of paper.

WRITING ABOUT IT   Use a separate piece of paper for your answers.

(1) Make up a poem about spring.

(2) Describe what you do when spring comes. If you do not have a special celebration, describe the things you like to do in the spring.

THE FIRST WOODPECKER

ABOUT THE PASSAGE   This is a Native American tale about how a human being was turned into a bird. Can you imagine why such a thing would happen?

REASON FOR READING   To find a message in the story.

READ THE PASSAGE

Many years ago the Great Spirit, **disguised** as an old man, came to the **wigwam** of a woman. Of course, the woman did not know who the visitor was.

The Great Spirit was very hungry and asked the woman for some food. The woman said she would bake a cake.

The woman made a little cake and baked it. When it was done, it was bigger than she thought it would be, so she decided to keep it for herself. She told the Great Spirit that she would make another cake.

The next cake she baked turned out even larger than the first one. "It is so large that I will keep it for a **feast,**" she thought. She told her **guest** that she would make still another cake.

The third cake was the largest of all. The woman did not know that the Great Spirit had used **magic** to make each cake larger. "I will not give away the largest cake of all," she thought.

So she told her guest that she did not have any food to give away. "You must go to the forest and look for food there," she said.

The Great Spirit, now very **angry,** said, "Men and women should be good and kind, but you are **selfish.** You will not be a human being any longer. You will live in the forests and hunt for your food in the bark of the trees."

The Great Spirit stamped one foot. The woman grew smaller and smaller. Wings and feathers grew from her body. With a loud cry, she flew away into the forests.

And to this day, all **woodpeckers** live in the forest and hunt for their food in the bark of trees.

THINKING IT OVER

(1) Why was the woman turned into a woodpecker?_____

_____

(2) How many cakes did she bake? _____

(3) What is the message of this old tale?_____

_____

STUDYING THE PASSAGE

(1) Find the Main Idea: Choose one.
   (a) How the Great Spirit became an old man.
   (b) How a woman baked some cakes.
   (c) How a woman was punished for her selfishness.
   (d) Why woodpeckers have to hunt for their food.   ____

(2) Find the Facts: Mark each one *true* or *false*.
   (a) The old man was very hungry.   (a) ____
   (b) The woman burned the first cake.   (b) ____
   (c) The woman gave the old man the last cake she made.   (c) ____
   (d) The woman told the old man to look for food in the forest. (d) ____
   (e) The Great Spirit became very angry.   (e) ____
   (f) When the Great Spirit stamped one foot, the woman did
       the opposite of what her cakes did when she baked them.   (f) ____

(3) Find the Order: Number the following in the order in which they appear
   in the passage.
   (a) The woman did not know who the old man was.   ____
   (b) This cake was so large that the woman thought she would keep
       it for a feast.   ____
   (c) She told her guest that she did not have any food to give away. ____
   (d) The woman did not know the Great Spirit had used magic to make
       each cake larger.   ____
   (e) The woman made a little cake and baked it.   ____

24

(4) Go beyond the Facts: Choose one.

    (a) Stories about animals are always for young people.

    (b) A simple story can be used to tell a serious thought or message.

    (c) Good stories always have a happy ending.

    (d) Good stories must always be true.   ____

USING THE WORDS

(1) Words and Their Meanings: Write the letter of the correct definition beside the word.

____ to disguise	(a)	a large meal
____ wigwam	(b)	the use of charms or special words to make mysterious, unexpected things happen
____ feast		
____ guest	(c)	large, arched or domed Native American dwelling
____ magic	(d)	feeling very mad
____ angry	(e)	to hide oneself by using a costume or mask
____ selfish	(f)	a bird with a strong, pointed bill that is used for drilling and pecking trees
____ woodpecker		
	(g)	a person who is visiting
	(h)	thinking only of oneself

(2) Write a paragraph using 2 of the vocabulary words. Use a separate piece of paper.

WRITING ABOUT IT   Use a separate piece of paper for your answers.

(1) Describe what you think the woman looked like before she was changed into a woodpecker. Choose your words carefully so your reader can "see" the woman.

(2) How would you describe "selfishness"? Give some examples of someone being selfish.

A GIRL AHEAD OF THE REST

ABOUT THE PASSAGE   A young African American became the fastest
woman runner in the world. Her success at run-
ning is very **impressive** because of her childhood
illnesses.

REASON FOR READING   To learn what made Wilma Rudolph an **inspiration** to so many people.

READ THE PASSAGE

Tall, straight, and strong, she stood on the winner's stand. The gold medal was hers! Few people, however, knew the problems Wilma Rudolph had overcome to win this treasure.

Wilma was one of twenty-two children and was only four and one half pounds when she was born. She walked later than the other children in her poor Tennessee town. When she was four, she had scarlet fever, double pneumonia, and polio. After this, she could not use her left leg, and the doctors said she might never walk again.

"Wilma will walk," her mother said. Every week, on her day off, Mrs. Rudolph took Wilma ninety miles on a bus to a clinic in Nashville. There she received treatment for her **paralyzed** leg. At home her family also **massaged** her **damaged** muscles.

When she was six, Wilma began to walk slowly and **awkwardly** with her leg in a brace. At eight, she limped around in a special heavy, high-built shoe. By the time she was thirteen, however, she was running and playing with the neighborhood children.

Wilma amazed everyone. In high school she joined the baseball, track, and basketball teams. She was called "Skeeter" because she seemed always to be flying around like a mosquito. She became the star attraction at her school's athletic events, and people said, "She runs like she was born to run." Wilma decided that she was born to win, too. In college at Tennessee State, she won meet after meet, although she was still sometimes sick.

Wilma ran with grace and **determination.** She beat all her **competitors** as

26

she did at the 1960 Olympics in Rome, Italy. Here the people hailed her as the "gazelle"* and shouted out words of encouragement. Wilma set new records in the 100-meter dash and the 200-meter dash, and she won the 400-meter relay with her teammates.

At twenty, Wilma Rudolph became the first American woman to win three Olympic gold medals in track and field. This was a great feat, especially because of all the problems she had to overcome.

Wilma Rudolph died young—at 54—in 1994.

THINKING IT OVER

(1) Why was Wilma Rudolph's success so impressive?_____

_____

(2) In what ways is Wilma Rudolph an inspiration to other people?_____

_____

STUDYING THE PASSAGE

(1) Find the Main Idea: Choose one answer.
   (a) Wilma was intelligent.
   (b) Wilma could do many things well.
   (c) Wilma's determination helped her be successful.
   (d) Wilma was handicapped.   ____

(2) Find the Facts: Mark each one *true* or *false*.
   (a) Even before she was sick, Wilma walked later than most
       children.   (a) ____
   (b) Wilma was the youngest of twenty children.   (b) ____
   (c) Wilma won four Olympic gold medals.   (c) ____
   (d) Wilma's left leg was paralyzed when she was a child.   (d) ____
   (e) Wilma's family helped her regain the use of her leg.   (e) ____
   (f) Wilma enjoyed figure skating in high school.   (f) ____

*A small, graceful antelope, which looks a little like a deer.

(3) Find the Order: Number the following in the order in which they appear in the passage.

(a) She began to walk slowly and awkwardly with her leg in a brace. _____

(b) After this, she could not use her left leg. _____

(c) Here people hailed her as the "gazelle." _____

(d) There she received treatment for her paralyzed leg. _____

(e) She was called "Skeeter." _____

(4) Go beyond the Facts: Choose *two*.

(a) Wilma probably was an outstanding student.

(b) You are more likely to succeed if you come from a big family.

(c) Wilma was good at many sports.

(d) Wilma's mother must have been a strong and dedicated woman. _____ _____

USING THE WORDS

(1) Words and Their Meanings: Write the letter of the correct definition beside the word.

_____ impressive	(a)	to rub with the hands
_____ inspiration	(b)	a mind made up to do something
_____ paralyzed	(c)	not able to move
_____ to massage	(d)	moving others to do more and better things
_____ damaged	(e)	outstanding
_____ awkwardly	(f)	rivals, people competing against one another
_____ determination	(g)	hurt
_____ competitors	(h)	clumsily, not gracefully

(2) Write a paragraph using 2 of the vocabulary words. Use a separate piece of paper.

WRITING ABOUT IT   Use a separate piece of paper to answer the questions.

(1) Describe the things that Wilma Rudolph had to overcome. Then explain what you think enabled her to succeed.

(2) Imagine you could not use your left leg. Describe some of the difficulties you would have.

THE GOOSE WITH THE GOLDEN EGGS

ABOUT THE PASSAGE

People tell stories for different reasons—to entertain, to surprise, to describe something that has happened. Sometimes they tell a story to teach a lesson or to give a message. Stories that do this are called **fables.**

REASON FOR READING

To learn what a fable is and to find out the writer's message in this story.

READ THE PASSAGE

In Selection 7, "Spring Celebrations," you learned how eggs are used as **symbols** in countries all over the world. In this story, an egg is again used to stand for something else. In this case, a beautiful golden egg is used to teach a lesson.

The story is really a **fable.** A fable is a story a writer uses to teach us something. See if you can **figure out** what the writer is teaching in this fable.

One day a **country** man looked in his goose's nest and found an egg, all yellow and **glittering.** When he held it up, it was as heavy as **lead.** He was going to **discard** it because he thought that someone had played a **trick** on him. But, on second thought, he took it home and soon found to his **delight** that it was an egg of pure gold.

Every morning the same thing **occurred,** and the man soon became **wealthy** by selling the eggs. As time passed, all the man could think about was getting more eggs and more money. Planning to get at one time all the gold the goose could give, the man killed the goose and opened it. Inside he found—nothing!

THINKING IT OVER

(1) What is a fable?_____

_____

(2) Why was the goose so unusual?_____

_____

(3) What is the writer really telling you in this story?_____

_____

STUDYING THE PASSAGE

(1) Find the Main Idea: Choose one.
    (a) Do not be content with just a little.
    (b) Never kill a goose.
    (c) Do not be greedy.
    (d) "Don't put all your eggs in one basket."   _____

(2) Find the Facts: Mark each one *true* or *false*.
    (a) There is more to the story than meets the eye.   (a) _____
    (b) As time passed, money became more and more important
         to the man.   (b) _____
    (c) The yellow and glittering egg was very light in weight.   (c) _____
    (d) Once a week the goose laid a golden egg.   (d) _____
    (e) The man grew rich.   (e) _____
    (f) He killed the goose because he was hungry.   (f) _____

(3) Find the Order: Number the following in the order in which they appear
    in the passage.
    (a) The man took the egg home.   _____
    (b) The man killed the goose.   _____
    (c) The man found an egg, all yellow and glittering.   _____
    (d) The man sold the eggs.   _____
    (e) This story is about a golden egg.   _____

(4) Go beyond the Facts: What *one* lesson does the story tell us?
    (a) You should never kill a goose.
    (b) You should not be greedy.
    (c) You can become rich by selling eggs.
    (d) You should read more fables.   _____

USING THE WORDS

(1) Words and Their Meanings: Write the letter of the correct definition beside the word.

____	fable	(a)	to determine, to conclude
____	to figure out	(b)	joy, pleasure
____	country	(c)	rich
____	glittering	(d)	a story that teaches a lesson
____	lead	(e)	shining
____	to discard	(f)	to throw away
____	trick	(g)	a very heavy metal
____	delight	(h)	to happen
____	to occur	(i)	an undeveloped part of the land—open space, few buildings
____	wealthy	(j)	something done to mislead or confuse

(2) Write a paragraph using 2 of the vocabulary words. Use a separate piece of paper.

WRITING ABOUT IT   Use a separate piece of paper for your answers.

(1) This story describes a yellow and glittering egg. Describe a regular egg that you buy in a store. Then explain the different ways it can be used, cooked, and eaten.

(2) Write a mystery story called "The Missing Golden Egg."

31

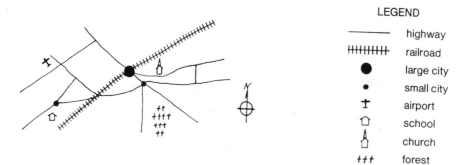

A DIFFERENT KIND OF LEGEND

ABOUT THE PASSAGE

You have probably read **legends** that tell stories of early time. The legend in this passage is a different kind, and yet it still tells a story.

REASON FOR READING

To find out how to read a map.

READ THE PASSAGE

Have you ever tried to find your way in a strange town? What do you usually do? Ask one of the **local** people?

I have tried asking people the way. Often, I am told something like this: "Well, you just walk down to Sarah's **studio.** Then continue up past the drug store and go left at the mailbox."

That is fine except I do not know which building is Sarah's studio. I find there are two drug stores and many mailboxes! Asking the way often does not work.

What does work to get you around **unfamiliar** territory is a map. To use a map, you must be able to read it. If you want to use a map, here's what you should do:

(1) First, find out which is north, south, east, and west.

(2) Next, look for the **special signs** and symbols on the map. This means you must find out what things stand for other things.

For example, a red line usually stands for a main highway or freeway. A black line stands for a street, and a black line with little lines across it (┼┼┼┼┼┼┼┼┼┼) stands for a railroad. A blue line usually stands for a river.

The size of cities is **indicated** by the size of a black dot (● ● •). An airport is shown by a tiny plane (✈).

All this **information** explain-

32

ing what the lines and shapes stand for is given in the "legend." It is called the legend because it *tells the story* of the map. The legend is usually found at the bottom of the map.

(3) Then, of course, in order to find your way, you must know where you are first. Mark this place on the map. Then, find the place on the map where you want to go and mark that. Now you can read the map to see what seems the best way to get to your **destination.** Read the map at the beginning of the passage and see if you can **identify** the different symbols.

THINKING IT OVER

(1) What is the legend in this passage? _____

_____

(2) What must you know before you can *read* a map? _____

(3) Draw a line on the map showing the best way to get from the church to the airport.

STUDYING THE PASSAGE

(1) Find the Main Idea: Choose one.
   (a) How to find your way in a strange town.
   (b) How to find an airport.
   (c) How to read a map.
   (d) What a "legend" is.   ____

(2) Find the Facts: Mark each one *true* or *false*.
   (a) To read a map you should know where north, south, east, and west are.   (a) ____
   (b) You could not read a map without the legend.   (b) ____
   (c) "Legend" is a good name because it tells the story of the map.   (c) ____
   (d) Cities are shown on the map by a tiny house.   (d) ____
   (e) You must know where you are on the map before you can find your way.   (e) ____
   (f) The map will probably show you several ways that you can get to the place you want to reach.   (f) ____

(3) Find the Order: Number the following in the order in which they appear in the passage.

(a) Mark the spot where you are. _____

(b) Decide the best way to go. _____

(c) Look at the legend to see what the signs and symbols mean. _____

(d) Mark the spot where you want to go. _____

(e) Look for north, south, east, and west on the map. _____

(4) Go beyond the Facts: Which does the writer suggest is the best way to find your way in a strange town?

(a) Ask one of the local people.

(b) Find the post office.

(c) Get hold of a local map.

(d) Follow the signs on the streets. _____

USING THE WORDS

(1) Words and Their Meanings: Write the letter of the correct definition beside the word. The first word has *two* meanings.

_____	legend	(a)	shown
_____		(b)	to recognize
_____	local	(c)	particular, distinctive
_____	studio	(d)	a room or building where an artist works
_____	unfamiliar	(e)	just in one city, community, or place
_____	special	(f)	a popular story handed down from earlier times
_____	signs	(g)	the place where a person is going
_____	indicated	(h)	an explanation of special signs that are used on a map
_____	information		
_____	destination	(i)	things that stand for something; also markers found on streets
_____	to identify	(j)	not known, strange
		(k)	knowledge, facts

(2) Write a paragraph using 2 of the vocabulary words. Use a separate piece of paper.

WRITING ABOUT IT   Use a separate piece of paper for your answers.

(1)   Draw a map showing your route to school. Be sure to show where north, south, east and west are located. Include enough symbols in your legend.

(2)   Describe your route to school in your own words. Point out special things of interest, so it is more of an adventurous journey than a daily chore.

THE BIGGEST LAND ANIMAL

ABOUT THE PASSAGE

Which is the biggest land animal that ever lived?

(a) an elephant   (c) a hippopotamus

(b) a rhinoceros   (d) none of the above

REASON FOR READING

To find out about this big animal. As you read, see how many words you can find that refer to size.

READ THE PASSAGE

We won't see these animals around today, which is just as well, because they were giants. Some were as tall as houses; some were as heavy as ten elephants; and others were nearly as long as six cars. Who were they? Dinosaurs.

Dinosaurs were the biggest land animals that ever **inhabited** the earth. They lived millions of years ago, long before people **populated** the world. They belong to the family of cold-blooded animals known as **reptiles.** This is the same family that alligators, crocodiles, lizards, and snakes belong to. The word "dinosaur" means "terrible lizard."

There were many different kinds of dinosaurs. Some of them were plant eaters. The huge *brontosaurus* was one of these. Its name means "thunder lizard." It was called this because its **massive** feet made a noise like thunder when it walked.

Other dinosaurs hunted meat to eat. *Tyrannosaurus rex* was the king of the hunters; that is why he was called "rex." The word *rex* means "king." *Tyrannosaurus rex* had huge teeth. They were as long as pencils and very, very sharp. What did these hunters eat? Other dinosaurs.

Some dinosaurs had a way of keeping safe from their hunting relatives. They had hard plates on their backs that were like **armor.** When danger was near, they just sat tight. One of these was *anky-losaurus* (an-KIE-luh-SOR-us). It also had a strong tail, which it could swing like a club.

Not all dinosaurs were enormous. There were some that were about the size of a chicken. Even the immense ones had small heads, though, and tiny brains.

There are many things we do not know about the dinosaurs. For example, what color were they? Scientists think they were brown or green, but they are not sure. The biggest question that has not been answered is, why did they die out?

Some say the dinosaurs became **extinct** because the world became too hot and burned their food. Others say the world became too cold, and they froze to death. Now scientists are saying perhaps a meteor came out of the sky and caused a **violent** explosion that covered the earth with dust and **debris.**

Whatever the reason, the only place we can come face to face with a dinosaur today is in a museum.

THINKING IT OVER

(1) What is the biggest animal that ever lived on land?_____

_____

(2) Why don't we see it today? _____

_____

(3) List five words that the writer uses to describe the size of this animal. _____

_____

_____

STUDYING THE PASSAGE

(1) Find the Main Idea: Choose one.
   (a) What it was like to live long ago.
   (b) Why we won't meet a dinosaur today.
   (c) Dinosaurs were of different sizes.
   (d) What the biggest land animals were like.   _____

(2) Find the Facts: Mark each one *true* or *false*.

    (a) Snakes, lizards, and crocodiles are reptiles like the dinosaur.   (a) ____

    (b) Dinosaurs were all meat-eaters.   (b) ____

    (c) The *brontosaurus* was called that because it sounded like thunder when it walked.   (c) ____

    (d) *Tyrannosaurus rex* had big teeth.   (d) ____

    (e) These enormous animals had tiny brains.   (e) ____

    (f) We do not know why dinosaurs died out.   (f) ____

(3) Find the Order: Number the following in the order in which they appear in the passage.

    (a) There were many different kinds of dinosaurs.

    (b) There are many things we do not know about dinosaurs.   ____

    (c) Other dinosaurs hunted meat to eat.   ____

    (d) Dinosaurs were the biggest animals that ever lived on land.   ____

    (e) Some had hard plates on their backs.   ____

(4) Go beyond the Facts: The writer describes the size of the biggest animal in all except *one* of the following ways. Which one?

    (a) She gives its height, length, and weight.

    (b) She gives details.

    (c) She compares the size of this animal with that of things you see every day.

    (d) She tells you why this animal is so big.   ____

USING THE WORDS

(1) Words and Their Meanings: Write the letter of the correct definition beside the word. *Two* words have the same definition.

    ____ inhabited   (a) showing or acting with great force

    ____ populated   (b) stopped living; died off

    ____ reptiles   (c) lived in or on

    ____ massive   (d) a covering that protects

    ____ armor   (e) very large

    ____ extinct   (f) broken remains

    ____ violent   (g) animals that crawl, whose body temperature changes to be

    ____ debris   the same as their surroundings, and whose skin is covered with scales or bony plates

(2) Write a paragraph using 2 of the vocabulary words. Use a separate piece of paper.

WRITING ABOUT IT   Use a separate piece of paper for your answers.

(1) Find out more about dinosaurs. Then write a report on them.

(2) Write about the animals in a zoo, using as many different words referring to size as you can.

Selection 13—Subject: Science
Theme: Getting to Know Yourself

MISS T.*

ABOUT THE PASSAGE

What makes people look the way they do? Why do some of us have brown eyes and some of us blue eyes? Why are some people tall and some short? This selection has an answer.

REASON FOR READING

To enjoy a poem that makes you think.

READ THE PASSAGE

It's a very odd thing—
    As odd as can be—
That whatever Miss T. eats
    Turns into Miss T.;
Porridge and apples,
    Mince, muffins, and **mutton,**
Jam, junket[1], and jumbles[2]
    Not a rap[3], not a button
It matters; the moment
    They're out of her plate,
Though shared by Miss Butcher
    And **sour** Mr. Bate;
Tiny and cheerful,
    And as neat as can be,
Whatever Miss T. eats
    Turns into Miss T.

        —Walter de la Mare

All people **require** food to keep them alive and growing. But does it strike you as odd that people who eat the same food don't look alike? Miss T. doesn't look like Miss Butcher, and neither of them looks like sour old Mr. Bate! Yet, there they are, all eating the same food!

[1]a kind of custard
[2]small sugared cakes
[3]not worth very much

*Permission to include "Miss T." by Walter de la Mare has been granted by The Literary Trustees of Walter de la Mare and the Society of Authors as their representative.

In order to understand why we all don't look alike, you have to know what our bodies are made of. Everything in our body is made up of tiny units called **cells.** The food we eat is broken down and changed into different kinds of cells. Cells are so small that we can see them only if we look through a **microscope.** Different parts of our bodies are made up of different kinds of cells. Our hair is made up of one kind, our skin of another, and our bones of yet another.

Inside each cell are even tinier things called **genes.** The genes tell each cell what to do. The genes in the cells in Miss T.'s hair tell those cells to look red. The genes in the cells in Mr. Bate's legs tell those cells how long to make his legs grow.

Most people have different genes. They look different from each other. The only people who **resemble** each other are **identical** twins. Why is this?

THINKING IT OVER

(1) What is the odd thing that happens when Miss T. eats her dinner? _____

_____

(2) Why do identical twins look like each other? _____

_____

STUDYING THE PASSAGE

(1) Find the Main Idea: Choose one.
   (a) We need food to live.
   (b) People do not look alike because they have different genes.
   (c) All cells have genes.
   (d) Miss T. is tiny and cheerful.   ____

(2) Find the Facts: Mark each one *true* or *false.*
   (a) Mr. Bate is tiny and cheerful.   (a) ____
   (b) You have to look through a microscope to see cells.   (b) ____

(c) Cells tell the genes how you should look. (c) _____

(d) Miss T. eats jam and muffins. (d) _____

(e) Everything in your body is made up of tiny units called cells. (e) _____

(f) Everyone has the same genes. (f) _____

(3) Find the Order: Number the following in the order in which they appear in the passage.

(a) Miss T. doesn't look like Miss Butcher.

(b) Inside of each cell are even tinier things called genes. _____

(c) "Tiny and cheerful, And as neat as can be." _____

(d) People have different genes. _____

(e) "Porridge and apples, Mince, muffins and mutton..." _____

(4) Go beyond the Facts: Rachel and Rebecca are identical twins. Which *one* of the following is probably *most* true about them?

(a) Rachel and Rebecca always eat exactly the same things.

(b) Rachel and Rebecca always sneeze at the same time.

(c) Rachel and Rebecca both have the same shaped noses.

(d) Rachel and Rebecca don't look alike. _____

USING THE WORDS

(1) Words and Their Meanings: Write the letter of the correct definition beside the word. One word has *two* meanings.

_____ mutton	(a)	units telling the body how to look
_____ sour	(b)	units making up everything in the body
_____	(c)	exactly the same
_____ require	(d)	must have
_____ cells	(e)	meat from grown-up sheep
_____ microscope	(f)	instrument that makes tiny things look bigger than they are
_____ genes		
_____ to resemble	(g)	tasting bad
_____ identical	(h)	cross; unpleasant
	(i)	to look like something else

(2) Write a paragraph using 2 of the vocabulary words. Use a separate piece of paper.

WRITING ABOUT IT   Use a separate piece of paper for your answers.

(1)   Write a paragraph explaining why Miss T. does not look like Miss Butcher or Mr. Bates.

(2)   Write a fun poem about identical twins.

HOW ROCKS ARE MADE

ABOUT THE PASSAGE

Many rocks are very old. They take a long time to form. Scientists study rocks to learn how they were made millions of years ago. From their study they can also learn a lot about how the earth was made.

REASON FOR READING

To learn three ways that rocks are formed.

READ THE PASSAGE

Have you ever **examined** the rocks you pass on the road to school each day or skip across the surface of a quiet pond? Not all rocks look alike, do they? They look different because they are made in different ways.

One way rocks are made is by cooling. Deep inside the earth it is so hot that everything is **molten. Solid** things change to **liquid** because it is so hot.

Sometimes this liquid pours out onto the surface of the earth from a **volcano.** When this liquid cools, it hardens into rock.

Another way rocks are made is by **pressure.** Long ago, much of what is now dry land was covered with water. Many plants and animals **lived in** the oceans. They fell to the bottom when they died. This happened for millions of years. Layer after layer of dead plants and animals piled on top of each other.

All these layers of things were very heavy. The plants and animals in the bottom layers got pressed together hardest. They got pressed together so hard that they became rock.

Other rocks are made from parts of rocks that already are formed. This is how it happens. High in the mountains it is cold all the time. Snow that falls there never melts. When it piles up very high, it turns to ice; it starts sliding very slowly down the mountain because it is so heavy. It rolls the rocks under it so hard that they get broken up into pieces. These rocks of all sizes are carried along by the ice. When the ice melts, they are left behind on the ground.

By studying rocks made in all three of these ways, scientists can learn more about how the earth was formed and how old it is.

THINKING IT OVER

(1) Why do scientists study rocks? _They study rocks because_
scientists can learn more about how the
Earth was formed and how obits

STUDYING THE PASSAGE

(1) Find the Main Idea: Choose one.
(a) Some rocks were made by snow.
(b) Rocks look different because they are made in different ways.
(c) Not all rocks look alike.
(d) Why volcanoes are dangerous

(2) Find the Facts: Mark each one *true* or *false*.
(a) It is very cold deep inside the earth.   (a) _F._
(b) Long ago, there was water on much of what is now dry land.   (b) _T._
(c) Some rocks get broken into pieces.   (c) _T._
(d) Snow high in the mountains never melts.   (d) _T._
(e) All rocks are made of dead plants and animals.   (e) _F._
(f) Some rocks are made from ice.   (f) _F._

(3) Find the Order: Number the following in the order in which they appear in the passage.
(a) Rocks of all sizes are carried along by the ice.   ____
(b) Sometimes the liquid pours out onto the surface of the earth. ____
(c) Not all rocks look alike.   ____
(d) Snow slides down the mountain.   ____
(e) Many plants and animals lived in the water.   ____

(4) Go beyond the Facts: Choose one.
(a) The three ways rocks are made are very different.
(b) The rocks formed when snow slides down a mountain are really made by pressure, too.
(c) The rocks that are cooled are made almost the same way as rocks made by pressure.
(d) Rocks made by cooling are harder than rocks made by pressure.   ____

USING THE WORDS

(1) Words and Their Meanings: Write the letter of the correct definition beside the word.

G. to examine
A. molten
d. solid
C. liquid
F. volcano
B. pressure
E. to live in

(a) force from something heavy
(b) made liquid by heat
(c) flowing freely like water
(d) keeping the same size and shape
(e) to inhabit
(f) an opening on the earth's surface from which pours a very hot liquid
(g) to look at closely

(2) Write a paragraph using 2 of the vocabulary words. Use a separate piece of paper.

WRITING ABOUT IT   Use a separate piece of paper for your answers.

(1) Describe in your own words the three ways rocks are made.

(2) Write a story about a magic rock.

ANTS

ABOUT THE PASSAGE

You may think ants and human beings are very different from each other. They certainly are different in **appearance** and size, but in other ways, they are **similar.**

REASON FOR READING

To discover in what ways ants and human beings are alike.

READ THE PASSAGE

Do you know that some insects are very much like people? They live together in crowded cities and work together for the good of all. Ants are insects of this kind. They are **social** insects, living together in **colonies.** They build their houses to **suit** the **climate** of the place where they live, and they live almost everywhere in the world.

Like people, ants **distribute** the work to be done. Some worker ants get food and feed it to young ants. They are like farmers gathering food for people to eat. When the young ants eat the food, they give out a liquid that the grown-up ants can eat. In some colonies, the ants feed liquid food to a few special workers. These workers store it in their stomachs, which become very large. They spend all their time in the nest giving out liquid to whoever needs it, just like the person who runs a store.

Ants are ruled by a queen ant. She spends all her time laying eggs, and the worker ants take care of her.

New queens come to rule a colony in many different ways. One kind of ant queen can go into another colony and kill the old queen. Another kind can take some workers with her from her mother's nest and start a new colony of her own. Another kind of ant queen takes her young with her and hides in some other colony. She gets some of the workers to feed her young instead of the old queen's young. In this way she becomes strongest in the colony, and she rules.

Some ants form armies and fight battles with other colonies, but not all ants are **fierce.** Some live in peace with their neighbors.

Ben Yabbon

THINKING IT OVER

(1) What is the role of the worker ant? _They help the queen._

_____

(2) Who rules the ants? _The queen of the ants do._

STUDYING THE PASSAGE

(1) Find the Main Idea: Choose one.
   (a) There are different kinds of ants.
   (b) Ants live very much like human beings. ✓
   (c) Ants live alone.
   (d) Ants live as long as human beings.

(2) Find the Facts: Mark each one _true_ or _false_.
   ✗ (a) Living and working together is called being social.   (a) F. T
   ✗ (b) Ants always build the same kinds of homes.   (b) T. F
   ✓ (c) In an ant city, different ants do different jobs.   (c) T.
   ✓ (d) Ants are ruled by a male.   (d) F.
   ✓ (e) In some ant colonies, elections are held to choose a new queen.   (e) F.
   ✓ (f) One kind of ant queen gets workers to feed her young.   (f) T.

(3) Find the Order: Number the following in the order in which they appear in the
    passage.
   (a) Some ants fight battles.   e.
   (b) Different groups of ants do different jobs.   c.
   (c) Ants live in colonies.   d.
   (d) New queens come to rule a colony in many different ways.   b.
   (e) Some insects are very much like people.   a.

(4) Go beyond the Facts: Which _one_ of the following is a way people are just like
    ants?
   ✗ (a) The young give off a liquid that the grown-ups eat.
      (b) They store liquid in their stomachs and give it to others.
      (c) Queens spend all their time making new citizens.
      (d) They build their houses to suit the climate.

48

USING THE WORDS

(1) Words and Their Meanings: Write the letter of the correct definition beside the word. One word has *two* meanings.

_h_	appearance	(a)	to be right for, to best fit
_c_	similar	(b)	the kind of weather that is usual in a certain place during a year
_d_	social		
_g_	colonies	(c)	groups of the same kind of animals or plants living together
_a_	suit		
_f_ Suit.		(d)	to divide and hand out
_b_	climate	(e)	wild; sharp and angry
_i_	to distribute	(f)	a set of clothes for outer wear
_e_	fierce	(g)	living together in groups
		(h)	the way something looks
		(i)	like something else in some way

(2) Write a paragraph using 2 of the vocabulary words. Use a separate piece of paper.

WRITING ABOUT IT   Use a separate piece of paper for your answers.

(1) Describe how ants and humans are alike. You need not write your facts in the same order as the writer of the passage, but be sure to make an outline before you start to write. Then you will have a definite plan to follow.

(2) Imagine a family of ants talking over their day. Describe what they tell each other. Use dialogue.

Selection 16—Subject: Science
Theme: The World of Water, Sea, and Fish

A DIFFICULT JOURNEY

ABOUT THE PASSAGE

Some fish are known for their size. Some (such as the shark and barracuda) are known for their meanness. Still others (such as the trout or the goldfish) are known for their beautiful color. Salmon are known for a special **quality** too—their toughness in a battle against great **difficulties.**

REASON FOR READING

To learn what difficulties salmon face and how they overcome them.

READ THE PASSAGE

Some fish spend all their lives in the place where they were born. Salmon do not. Born in the fresh water of rivers, they **migrate** to the ocean when young, then go back to the rivers as adults.

When fall comes, it is time for salmon to **spawn.** They leave the ocean and travel to the beginning of the river, where they were **hatched.** Sometimes these trips are more than 2,000 miles. On the long journey they have to fight against the **current** of the stream. Sometimes they even leap up waterfalls. When they reach the beginning of the river, they are often very tired and worn out from their long and difficult journey.

But they cannot rest. The mother fish makes a nest in the sand on the bottom of the river by slapping the sand with her tail. In this nest the mother lays her eggs and the father leaves his sperm. Then the mother covers the nest with sand and leaves the baby fish to hatch.

Some kinds of salmon are so worn out from their trip that they die after they spawn. Others swim back down the river and make the trip again the next fall.

The young fish hatch in the winter. Some **species** of salmon start the journey down the river to the ocean when they are a few inches long. They seem to be swimming backwards, but they are really carried downstream by the current. Others live in the river for two or three years before going to the ocean. All of these salmon, however, will make the trip back to where they first lived.

50

THINKING IT OVER

(1) Why do salmon leave the ocean and swim up rivers? _I think because_
they do it to spwam.

(2) Why is the salmon's journey difficult? _It is Because_
they get very tierd it is 2 00 miles.

STUDYING THE PASSAGE

(1) Find the Main Idea: Choose one.
   (a) How the mother salmon makes her nest.
   (b) How salmon jump up waterfalls.
   (c) How salmon make their young.
   (d) How young salmon swim backwards.

   _____

(2) Find the Facts: Mark each one *true* or *false*.
   (a) Salmon stay in one place all the time.   (a) F
   (b) The fall is the time for salmon to lay eggs.   (b) F
   (c) The father fish makes the nest.   (c) F
   (d) The nest is made in the sand.   (d) T
   (e) The current helps salmon in their journey up the river. (e) T
   (f) Salmon always go back to the place they were hatched to lay
       their eggs.   (f) T

(3) Find the Order: Number the following in the order in which they appear in the
    passage.
   (a) They leave the ocean and travel far up river.   e
   (b) Some salmon, when a few inches long, swim down the river.   b
   (c) They jump up waterfalls.   c
   (d) Some salmon die after spawning.   d
   (e) Salmon migrate.   a

The Samond's
journey is
diffacult
because
they
miles swim 2,000

(4) Go beyond the Facts: How does the author tell us about salmon?

    (a) She describes what salmon looks like.

    (b) She imagines what salmon like to eat.

    (c) She compares salmon with other fish.

    (d) She explains how salmon have their young.   _____

USING THE WORDS

(1) Words and Their Meanings: Write the letter of the correct definition beside the word.

_____ quality	(a) a steady movement of water
_____ difficulty	(b) to move from one place to another when seasons change
_____ to migrate	
_____ to spawn	(c) a necessary part of something
_____ to hatch	(d) a group of plants or animals that are like each other in certain ways
_____ current	(e) to break out of an egg
_____ species	(f) a hard thing to do
	(g) to lay fish eggs

(2) Write a paragraph using 2 of the vocabulary words. Use a separate piece of paper.

WRITING ABOUT IT   Use a separate piece of paper for your answers.

(1) Describe how salmon have their young.

(2) Like salmon, we all face difficulties in life. Describe a difficulty you have, or have had, and explain how you have dealt with it.

A NOISY BIRD

ABOUT THE PASSAGE

Some birds are quiet. Some birds sing lovely songs. Other birds make a **distinctive** noise for which they are best known. Do you know one that does this?

REASON FOR READING

To notice how the writer talks to you. She makes you feel that you can really hear the bird and see it at work in a tree.

READ THE PASSAGE

Listen! Can you hear it? You think it's a **carpenter** hammering in nails? No-o-o, look up there in that tree. What do you see? Yes, a bird! A very **peculiar** bird, I'd say. Most birds just sit in trees. But watch! This one is hopping up the side of the tree and putting its head on one side every now and then.

The bird is listening for insects. Ah, it's heard some. Look at it leaning back on its **stiff** tail. There! See how it makes that funny noise? Rat-tat-tat, goes the bird's sharp, pointed beak. Look! It certainly didn't take it very long to peck away the bark of the tree and make that hole in the trunk. There goes its long, sticky tongue into the hole. There must be a colony of insects in this tree. Insects are what this bird eats for supper.

Look over there! There's a big hole in the tree. That's where the bird's nest is. It must have found a **knot** in the tree trunk where a branch had been cut off. It hammered and picked at it until it made a hole big enough for a nest. Listen! There it goes again. Look! Here comes another bird! It must be the mate who heard the noise and came flying. They're **settling down** in the nest together to raise a family.

Do you know the name of this bird? Actually, it has several names. Some people call it the carpenter bird or the hammerhead (I bet you know why that is!), but most people call it the woodpecker.

THINKING IT OVER

(1)   What kind of noise does the woodpecker make? _____

(2)   How does it make the noise? _____

(3)   What is it doing? _____

_____

STUDYING THE PASSAGE

(1)   Find the Main Idea: Choose one.
    (a)   How a woodpecker makes noise.
    (b)   How a woodpecker finds its supper.
    (c)   How a woodpecker makes a nest.
    (d)   How a woodpecker calls its mate.   ____

(2)   Find the Facts: Mark each one *true* or *false*.
    (a)   The woodpecker walks up trees.   (a) ____
    (b)   It can hear very well.   (b) ____
    (c)   It often puts its head on one side.   (c) ____
    (d)   It uses its long, sticky tongue to get insects out of the tree.   (d) ____
    (e)   It knocks on wood when it wants its mate.   (e) ____
    (f)   Woodpeckers have several names.   (f) ____

(3)   Find the Order: Number the following in the order in which they appear in the passage.
    (a)   The bird is listening.   ____
    (b)   The bird eats insects for supper.   ____
    (c)   What an odd bird.   ____
    (d)   Some people call it the carpenter bird.   ____
    (e)   Its long, sticky tongue goes into the hole.   ____

(4)   Go beyond the Facts: The writer tells you which *one* of the following?
    (a)   Woodpeckers are large birds.
    (b)   Woodpeckers are black.
    (c)   Woodpeckers make nests in the spring.
    (d)   Woodpeckers eat insects that live beneath the bark of trees.   ____

USING THE WORDS

(1) Words and Their Meanings: Write the letter of the correct definition beside the word. One word has *two* meanings.

_____ distinctive   (a) odd, not usual or ordinary

_____ carpenter   (b) different from others in special ways

_____ peculiar   (c) pieces of string or cord tied together in a certain way

_____ stiff   (d) to make a home

_____ knot   (e) person who makes useful things, such as chairs, out of wood

_____

_____ to settle down (f) not easily bent or moved

                      (g) a hard place on a tree from which a branch grows

(2) Write a paragraph using 2 of the vocabulary words. Use a separate piece of paper.

WRITING ABOUT IT   Use a separate piece of paper for your answers.

(1) Find out more about the woodpecker or another bird you like. Then write about it.

(2) Describe a fly buzzing around your room to a friend you are talking to on the phone. Choose words that will help your friend "see" and "hear" your visitor.

MAKING THE WORLD FLAT

ABOUT THE PASSAGE

If you wanted to find a place in the world, such as the Arctic, which of the following would give you the most **accurate** location?

(a)   A **map.**

(b)   A **globe.**

(c)   It would not make any difference if you used either a map or a globe.

REASON FOR READING

To find out about globes and maps. Also, to think through a problem and come to a **conclusion.**

READ THE PASSAGE

If you want to find out where a place is located, the best place to look is on a globe. This is because, unlike a map, a globe is round, like the world itself. The problem with a globe is that it is **cumbersome.** It is not handy to carry around, and it is difficult to put in a book. So, instead, we make do with maps. We flatten the world, so we can stuff it in our pockets or study it in a book. How is this done? There are two ways.

The first way to make the world look flat is to cut it up. Try it with a **hollow** paper ball. You make the ball flat by starting at one **pole** (end), making three cuts to the **equator,** and a fourth cut almost in a complete circle through the other **pole.** Then lay the paper out flat, and it will look like the cut up map above.

This map lets us see all the world at once, but it is difficult to read,

especially if we want to study or measure the places that are cut through. Another problem is that the distances are not completely accurate.

The second way to make the world flat is to stretch it out. This produces a better map because the world is not cut up. But notice how the poles (the ends or top and bottom) of the world are stretched out. Also, some places look bigger than they really are. Can you tell what they are? To help you answer this question, look at the lines that go across the map at the top of this page. Then look at the lines that go across this map.

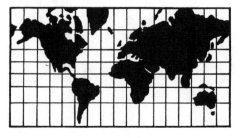

THINKING ABOUT IT

(1) List two ways the world can be made to look flat.

   (a) _____

   (b) _____

(2) Which places seem bigger on the second map? _____

   _____

(3) Why do these places look bigger? _____

   _____

STUDYING THE PASSAGE

(1) Find the Main Idea: Choose one.
   (a) Why the world is really flat.
   (b) How the world is round.
   (c) How to see the world all in one look.
   (d) Why some countries are bigger than others.   _____

(2) Find the Facts: Mark each one *true* or *false*.
   (a) A globe is more like the world than a map.   _____
   (b) You can cut up a hollow paper ball and make it flat.   _____
   (c) A map made by cutting up the world cannot be used to measure
       and study some places.   _____
   (d) The horizontal lines on the second map get closer together
       as they go towards the middle.   _____
   (e) On some maps, places look bigger than they really are.   _____

(3) Find the Order: Number the following in the order in which they appear in the
   passage.
   (a) This produces a better map because the world is not cut up.   _____
   (b) To help you answer the question, look at the lines which go across
       the map.   _____
   (c) The problem with a globe is that it is cumbersome.   _____

(d)　This map lets us see all the world at once.　　　＿＿＿

(e)　You can make the ball flat by starting at one pole.　＿＿＿

(4)　Go beyond the Facts: Which one is wrong?

　　(a)　You can make a perfect map of the world.

　　(b)　You cannot make a flat map that is just like the world.

　　(c)　The two maps show the world differently.

　　(d)　There are different ways to make a flat map of the world.　＿＿＿

USING THE WORDS

(1)　Words and Their Meanings: Write the letter of the correct definition beside the word. One word has *two* meanings.

＿＿＿ accurate	(a)	not solid; having a space inside
＿＿＿ map	(b)	pictures showing parts of an area (like the surface of the earth)
＿＿＿ globe		
＿＿＿ conclusion	(c)	free from mistakes, correct
＿＿＿ cumbersome	(d)	hard to handle or deal with
＿＿＿ hollow	(e)	an imaginary line which goes around the middle of the earth
＿＿＿ pole		
＿＿＿	(f)	final decision
＿＿＿ equator	(g)	round model of the earth
	(h)	either end of the earth
	(i)	a long stick

(2)　Write a paragraph using 2 of the words. Use a separate piece of paper.

WRITING ABOUT IT　Use a separate piece of paper for your answers.

(1)　Copy a map of the world. It may be the "cut up" kind or the "stretched out" kind. Then color in the two poles, the countries on the equator, the United States and the oceans to the west and east of it, a mountain, and a river.

(2)　It is fun studying the places on a map. But it is more fun to visit them. Describe a place you would like to visit and why you would like to go there.

Selection 19—Subject: Philosophy, Logic, and Language
Theme: The Why and How of It

WHAT IS BIG AND WHAT IS SMALL?

ABOUT THE PASSAGE   If you were asked to describe the size of a whale, you would probably say it was big. A pin, on the other hand, you would call small. But would an **elf** answer these questions in the same way?

REASON FOR READING   To think about how we decide what is big and what is small.

READ THE PASSAGE
The Little Elf*

I met a little Elf-man, once
Down where the lilies blow.
I asked him why he was so small
And why he didn't grow.

He **slightly** frowned and with his eye
He looked me through and through.
'I'm quite as big for me,' said he,
'As you are big for you.'

—John Kendrick Bangs

Have you ever stopped to think about how we talk about the size of things? I am sure you have often said something was as tiny as a **speck** of dust or as **immense** as an elephant, but just how small and how big were these things you were describing? Do you think the speck of dust would be as small to the elf in the poem as it would be to us? Would the elephant seem to be as big to the elf as a skyscraper does to us?

We usually **talk about** the size of things by **comparing** them to our own size or the size of something else. Thus, we think elephants, mountains, and oceans are big because they are bigger than we are and bigger than mice, hills, and brooks. We think elves, kittens, and specks of dust are small because they are smaller than we are. Dust would still be small to the elf, but a kitten would probably seem big to the elf because it would **tower over** him.

Then why does the elf say "I'm quite as big for me....As you are big for you?" It is because, again, he is comparing things to his own size. His stomach, heart, head, and legs are all smaller than ours are and the whole of his body is smaller than our body is. Thus, his legs and arms seem "quite as big" to him as our legs and arms seem big to us.

THINKING IT OVER

(1) How do we judge the size of things? _____

_____

STUDYING THE PASSAGE

(1) Find the Main Idea: Choose one.
   (a) How elves are really the same size as humans.
   (b) How sizes can seem different to different people.
   (c) How sizes can change.
   (d) How to make an elf angry.   _____

(2) Find the Facts: Mark each one *true* or *false*.
   (a) The poet thought the elf was small.   (a) _____
   (b) We say things are small when they are smaller than we are.   (b) _____
   (c) Things which seem small to us may seem big to other creatures.   (c) _____
   (d) The elf said he was the same size as the poet.   (d) _____
   (e) The parts of the elf's body seemed just as big to him as the
        parts of our body seem to us.   (e) _____
   (f) The elf's heart is the same size as a human's heart.   (f) _____

(3) Find the Order: Number the following in the order in which they appear in the passage.

(a) The elf frowned. —

(b) Would a speck of dust seem smaller to an elf than it does to you? —

(c) The poet said he met a little elf-man. —

(d) The whole of an elf's body is smaller than ours is. —

(e) Dust would still be small to an elf. —

(4) Go beyond the Facts: This passage tells *all but* which *one* of these?

(a) How we measure things.

(b) Why an elf seems just as big to himself as we do to ourselves.

(c) Why some things can seem big to one person and small to another.

(d) Why we grow to the size we do. —

USING THE WORDS

(1) Words and Their Meanings: Write the letter of the correct definition beside the word.

_	elf	(a)	a small spot
_	slightly	(b)	to see how alike and how different two things are
_	speck	(c)	to discuss; to remark on
_	immense	(d)	only a little, to a small degree
_	to talk about	(e)	a magical being who looks like a small person
_	compare	(f)	very big
_	to tower over	(g)	to be much taller than something else

(2) Write a paragraph using 2 of the vocabulary words. Use a separate piece of paper.

WRITING ABOUT IT   Use a separate piece of paper for your answers.

(1) Describe something that seems very small to you, but would be very large to an ant. Do not say what you are describing. Then give your description to a classmate and see if he or she can guess what is it is.

(2) Elves are magical little creatures. Write a story that has an elf in it.

Selection 20—Subject: Philosophy, Logic, and Language
Theme: Life and Its Meaning

PANDORA

ABOUT THE PASSAGE

Pandora opened a box and let out all the troubles into the world. This made her very unhappy. But there was something left in the box that would help her and all other human beings when they were troubled or unhappy.

REASON FOR READING

To read a very old tale that gives one explanation of why life is not always happy and carefree.

READ THE PASSAGE

A Greek god named Zeus gave Pandora a beautiful box as a wedding present, but he told Pandora that she must never open the box.

Every day Pandora **gazed** at the box happily. It was as bright as gold and **sparkled** in the sun, but soon she became tired of just looking at it. She began to **wonder** more and more what could be inside the box.

One day she became so **curious** that she decided she would have to open the box. She lifted the lid very carefully. Much to her surprise, out flew many tiny **spirits.** She slammed the lid down, but she was too late. All the cares, **woes,** and sicknesses that had been inside the box flew out through the open window. They went into the world to trouble human beings forever more.

Pandora did not know what to do. While she was thinking, she heard a noise coming from inside the box. Gently, she lifted the lid and looked inside. There, hanging from the gold rim around the lid was a beautiful little creature. It had colorful rainbow wings, but they looked as though they were broken. Pandora knew at once that the name of this creature was Hope.

Pandora **caressed** the creature to bring it back to life. As she did this, Hope crept into her heart. Since that day, it is Hope that has helped people to **overcome** their troubles.

62

THINKING IT OVER

(1) What did Pandora find that will always help us when we are in trouble? _____

_____

(2) How can it help us?_____

_____

STUDYING THE PASSAGE

(1) Find the Main Idea: Choose one.
   (a) How Zeus made Pandora unhappy.
   (b) Curiosity killed the cat.
   (c) How Pandora changed the world.
   (d) The story of a beautiful box.   _____

(2) Find the Facts: Mark each one *true* or *false*.
   (a) A Greek god gave Pandora the box.   (a) _____
   (b) Pandora opened the box because Zeus told her to.   (b) _____
   (c) When she opened the box, many tiny birds flew out.   (c) _____
   (d) Only four creatures were in the box.   (d) _____
   (e) The creatures flew out of the window into the world.   (e) _____
   (f) The last creature to come out of the box had been hurt. (f) _____

(3) Find the Order: Number the following in the order in which they appear in the passage.
   (a) Pandora became so curious that she opened the box.   _____
   (b) Pandora found a creature with rainbow wings.   _____
   (c) All the cares, woes, and sicknesses flew out of the box.   _____
   (d) Every day Pandora looked at the box happily.   _____
   (e) Zeus gave Pandora the box.   _____

(4) Go beyond the Facts: Which *one* is true according to the tale?
   (a) The world has always had troubles.
   (b) Look in a box if you are in trouble; it will help you.
   (c) The beautiful creature left in the box is a symbol for hope.
   (d) You should open boxes carefully because you don't always know what may be inside.   _____

USING THE WORDS

(1) Words and Their Meanings: Write the letter of the correct definition beside the word.

____	to gaze	(a)	to shine brightly
____	to sparkle	(b)	to want to know, to think about
____	to wonder	(c)	wanting to know, eager to learn
____	curious	(d)	to hug or hold closely, to cuddle
____	spirit	(e)	a magical creature
____	woes	(f)	sorrows
____	to caress	(g)	to look at
____	to overcome	(h)	to conquer

(2) Write a paragraph using 2 of the vocabulary words. Use a separate piece of paper.

WRITING ABOUT IT   Use a separate piece of paper for your answers.

(1) Describe what you think the world was like before Pandora let the spirits out of the box.

(2) Besides hope, what else do you think helps people in trouble?

BIG WORDS INTO SMALL

ABOUT THE PASSAGE

Some words seem impossible to pronounce, spell, or understand. But often they are not that difficult to figure out. You just need a little know-how. This passage gives you some suggestions.

REASON FOR READING

To learn some ways to make **pronouncing,** spelling, and understanding long words easier.

READ THE PASSAGE

I always hated it when people asked me where I lived. It was not that I did not like my home town, but just that it was called Panfromifwecanton!* Few people believed there was such a place, and even fewer people could say it.

Actually, it is quite easy to pronounce. All you have to do is to break it into **syllables:** pan-from-if-we-can-ton. A syllable is a small **unit** of sound built around a single **vowel** sound.

The vowels are *a, e, i, o, u* (and *y* when it sounds like an *i*).

Words with one syllable are *cat, dog, pen, all.*

Words with two syllables are *pen-cil, al-ways.*

Most words can be pronounced by breaking them into syllables. That is why Mary Poppins found it so very easy to say the word *supercalifragilisticexpialidocius.* Can you say it? Try! Now try pronouncing these words.

Remember to break them into syllables first: *development, encyclopedia, enchilada, parenthesis, irremovable.*

Breaking a word into smaller parts can also help you to spell the word correctly. You pay attention to each sound, rather than slurring them together.

As well as breaking a word down into its sounds, you can break a word down into its units of meaning. For example, sometimes you will find that a long word is made up of smaller words you already know, such as *overcoat, raindrop, shipwreck, handbag.*

A word can be broken down into three main parts: a **prefix,** which comes at the beginning; a **root,** or base, which is the main part of the word; and a **suffix,** which comes at the end. The trick here is knowing what they mean because a lot of them come from Latin and Greek.

Some prefixes that you probably

*This is a town in Wales, Great Britain.

know are *re*—again, *pre*—before, *anti*—against, *non*, *ir*, and *il*—not, *bi*—two, *trans*—across.

Some roots are *script*—to write, *port*—to carry, *ject*—to throw, *spec*—to see.

Some suffixes are *s*, *less*, *ful*, and *ize*. When they are added to a word, they change the meaning in some way, for example: *dog*, *dogs*; *help*, *helpless*; *cup*, *cupful*; *real*, *realize*.

When you see a long word, don't worry. Look at it carefully, break it down, and you'll figure it out.

THINKING IT OVER

(1) See if you can break the following words into syllables.

supercalifragilisticexpialidocius _____

opportunity _____

determination _____

(2) Give the meaning of these words.

inspector _____   transport _____

recycle _____   a script _____

bicycle _____   illegal _____

careless _____   reject _____

STUDYING THE PASSAGE

(1) Find the Main Idea: Choose one.
  (a) How difficult words are in the English language.
  (b) Conquering words by breaking them down.
  (c) How words are made up of syllables.
  (d) Why foreigners find the English language difficult.   ____

(2) Find the Facts: Mark each one *true* or *false*.

(a) To help pronounce a word, first break it into syllables. (b) _____

(b) Syllables are built around a vowel. (b) _____

(c) *A, e, i, o, u*, are the only vowels. (c) _____

(d) A word can be broken down into units of meaning. (d) _____

(e) A word has four main parts. (e) _____

(f) *Re, pre*, and *bi* are prefixes. (f) _____

(3) Find the Order: Number the following in the order in which they appear in the passage.

(a) You can break a word down into units of meaning. _____

(b) It was not that I did not like my hometown. _____

(c) When you see a long word, don't worry. _____

(d) A syllable is a small unit of sound. _____

(e) Breaking a word down can also help you to spell the word correctly. _____

(4) Go beyond the Facts: Which *two* are true?

(a) There is no logical pattern in the formation of our words.

(b) There is a logical pattern in the formation of our words.

(c) The meaning of long words is often determined by the meaning of the short words they are made from.

(d) You cannot understand long words unless you use the dictionary. ____ ____

USING THE WORDS

(1) Words and Their Meanings: Write the letter of the correct definition beside the word.

____ to pronounce (a) name for the letters *a, e, i, o, u* and sometimes *y*

____ syllables (b) a group of things taken as one

____ unit (c) small groups of sound built around a single vowel

____ vowel (d) to say out loud

____ prefix (e) the main part of a word

____ root (f) the end part of a word

____ suffix (g) the first part of a word

(2) Write a paragraph using 2 of the vocabulary words. Use a separate piece of paper.

WRITING ABOUT IT   Use a separate piece of paper for your answers.

(1) Reread the passage. Then make notes for the future on how to tackle long words.

(2) This selection is all about words. Choose a topic that interests you and have fun. Use words in new ways; put unusual words together; think of words with interesting sounds as well as meanings.

A HISTORY OF NUMERALS

ABOUT THE PASSAGE

Today we use numbers all the time. But a long, long time ago, people did not use numbers. When people began to count, they began to use numbers. Different cultures developed different ways of writing numbers.

REASON FOR READING

To learn about different ways of writing numbers.

READ THE PASSAGE

Imagine a world without numbers. How would you know what time it is or how old you are? How would you count the number of people in your class or in your family? Numbers help us **describe** things and people.

The way people use numbers has changed over the years. The earliest people didn't have many words for numbers. They had words for one, two, and many. People probably began to use numbers when they began to farm and herd animals. Then they had to keep track of their crops and their animals, so they invented numbers. They probably counted on their fingers. Later, they wrote down **numerals**, which are symbols for numbers.

Today, most people use numerals with these ten **digits**:

0 1 2 3 4 5 6 7 8 9

Numerals written with these digits are called Arabic numerals. This way of writing numbers was started in Asia, almost two thousand years ago. Then, about five hundred years later, it was brought to Europe.

In **ancient** times, there were many other numerals that different **cultures** used. For example, the ancient Egyptians and ancient Romans each had a different way of writing numbers.

Ancient Egyptians used the numeral ‖ for 1, ∩ for 10 and ? for 100.

69

Ancient Egyptian Numerals

| = 1

∩ = 10

? = 100

They could write other numbers between 1 and 100 with these numerals. If they wanted to write down the number 2, they would write || because 1 + 1 = 2. For the number 12, they would write ∩|| because 10 + 2 = 12. The order of Egyptian numerals does not matter. They could write ∩||, ||∩, or |∩| for 12. The ancient Romans used the numeral I for 1, V for 5, X for 10, and C for 100. To write numbers between 1 and 100, they used only these numerals.

Ancient Roman Numerals

I = 1

V = 5

X = 10

C = 100

When ancient Romans wrote the number 2, they wrote II. For the number 12, they wrote XII because 10 + 2 = 12. With Roman numerals, the order makes a difference. For example, XI = 11 because 10 + 1 = 11. But IX = 9 because 10 – 1 = 9. If the smaller numeral is in front, you subtract instead of add.

THINKING IT OVER

(1) Write two ways in which Egyptian numerals are different from Roman numerals.

_____

_____

STUDYING THE PASSAGE

(1) Find the Main Idea: Choose one.
   (a) People didn't use numbers long ago.
   (b) There are diferent ways to write numbers.
   (c) Ancient Egyptians had the best way to write numbers.
   (d) Most people write numbers with Arabic numberals. ____

(2) Find the Facts: Mark each one *true* or *false*.
   (a) There is no difference between Egyptian and Roman numerals. (a) ____
   (b) In Egyptian numerals, ∩| is the numeral for 11. (b) ____
   (c) In Roman numerals, IV stands for a different number than VI. (c) ____
   (d) People probably began to use numbers higher than three when they began to farm and herd animals. (d) ____

(3) Find the Order: Number the following in the order in which they appear in the passage.

(a) For the number 12, they would write ∩|| . _____

(b) The earliest people didn't have many words for numbers. _____

(c) Imagine a world without numbers. _____

(d) Arabic numerals were first used in Asia. _____

(e) With Roman numerals, the order makes a difference. _____

(4) Go beyond the Facts: Which *one* sentence is wrong?

(a) There is no symbol for the number 10 in Roman numerals.

(b) Egyptian, Roman, and Arabic numerals are the only kinds of numerals.

(c) 1, 10, and 100 are the only numbers that can be written with Egyptian numerals.

(d) Arabic numerals have ten digits. _____

USING THE WORDS

(1) Words and Their Meanings: Write the letter of the correct definition beside the word.

____ to describe	(a)	the way of life of a certain people at a certain time
____ digit	(b)	a symbol that stands for a number
____ numeral	(c)	to tell or write about in detail
____ ancient	(d)	of times from long ago
____ culture	(e)	the numerals 0 1 2 3 4 5 6 7 8 9

(2) Write a paragraph using 2 of the vocabulary words. Use a separate piece of paper.

WRITING ABOUT IT   Use a separate piece of paper for your answers.

(1) Write two Arabic numerals. Then write the same numbers in Egyptian and Roman numerals.

(2) Why do you think most people today use Arabic numerals instead of Egyptian or Roman numerals?

NUMBERS

ABOUT THE PASSAGE

Numbers are all around us. Our house or apartment has a number; the year we were born is a number; the score of a football game is a number. But can you actually see a number? See if you can answer the question after you have read the passage.

REASON FOR READING

To find out about numbers and to identify four ways people use numbers.

READ THE PASSAGE

We work with figures and numbers every day of our lives, not only in math class, but in many other ways. When we pay for something, we have to figure out the numbers to make sure we pay the right amount. Dad has to use numbers to pay for the groceries. Mom uses numbers to balance the checkbook. You have to use numbers to tell someone which grade you are in.

We use numbers in many different ways, but we never actually see them! This is because a number is an **idea.** A number stands for something that is in our mind.

Numbers are important to people for at least four reasons.

First, numbers **express** how many; for example, Li-ching has three pink mice. When numbers are used to tell how many, they are called **cardinal numbers.**

Second, numbers can say which one; for example, Emily was second in the race. These numbers are called **ordinal numbers** because they give the order.

Third, numbers show the **measurement** of things; for example, Juan caught a five-foot fish.

Fourth, numbers are used to group things; for example, Susan will trade eight pieces of gum for two candy bars. Things grouped together are called **sets.**

We use the signs [   ] to show how many items are in a set. For example:

[]   stands for 3 mice.

Look at these sets:

[😊 😊 😊 😊]   []

happy people   unhappy people

THINKING IT OVER

(1) Can you see a number? _____

(2) How many happy people are there in the drawing above? _____

(3) How many groups or sets are shown above? _____

(4) Give the ordinal number which tells which set the mice are in. _____

_____

STUDYING THE PASSAGE

(1) Find the Main Idea: Choose one.
    (a) Numbers are used in mathematics.
    (b) How to see a number.
    (c) How numbers stand for ideas in mathematics.
    (d) Numbers tell us "how many."   ____

(2) Find the Facts: Mark each one *true* or *false*.
    (a) We are using numbers all the time in our daily lives.   (a) ____
    (b) We use numbers in many different ways.   (b) ____
    (c) When you say you have three meals a day, you are using
         cardinal numbers.   (c) ____
    (d) Ordinal numbers tell you how many.   (d) ____
    (e) Things grouped together are called sets.   (e) ____
    (f) The signs [   ] are used to show sets.   (f) ____

(3) Find the Order: Number the following in the order in which they appear in the passage.

(a) A number stands for something in our mind.

(b) Numbers show the measurement of things. ____

(c) When we pay for something, we have to figure out numbers. ____

(d) Numbers group things. ____

(e) Numbers are important to people for at least four reasons. ____

(4) Go beyond the Facts: Which *one* is wrong?

(a) When we say we need two more yards of material, we are using numbers to measure.

(b) When we say, "I want three feet of yarn," we are using numbers to say how many.

(c) When we say, "Mr. Kobos has a big car, and Ms. Perez has a small car," we are using numbers to group.

(d) When we say, "Terry came in first in class," we are using numbers to say which one. ____

USING THE WORDS

(1) Words and Their Meanings: Write the letter of the correct definition beside the word.

____ idea   (a) something in your mind; a thought
____ to express   (b) the size of something said in numbers
____ cardinal number   (c) to state or say; to make known
____ ordinal number   (d) a collection of things, a number of things put together
____ measurement   (e) number that tells how many
____ set   (f) number that tells which one

(2) Write a paragraph using 2 of the vocabulary words. Use a separate piece of paper.

WRITING ABOUT IT   Use a separate piece of paper for your answers.

(1) Explain the four ways people use numbers. Give an example of each one.

(2) Some people think that the number seven is lucky. Write a story describing how the number seven brought good luck to a homeless child.

MEASURING GROWTH

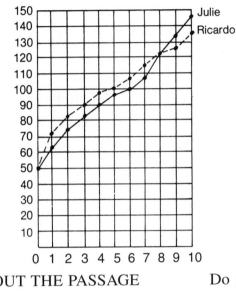

Numbers on side of graph are centimeters.
Numbers on bottom of graph are years.
— — — This line shows Ricardo's growth.
———— This line shows Julie's growth.

ABOUT THE PASSAGE

Do you keep track of how much you grow each year? Many people do. Some make marks on the kitchen door; others write it down in a diary; others make a **graph.** This is what Julie and Ricardo did.

REASON FOR READING

To learn how to make a graph to measure growth.

READ THE PASSAGE

Julie and Ricardo are sitting on Ricardo's steps one day. They are talking about school. Julie tells Ricardo that the whole class is going to be measured by the nurse at the beginning of next week. Ricardo says that he is measured by his mother **annually** on his birthday. Julie says that her father does the same thing. The two children decide to compare how they had grown from the day they were born. They are both ten years old now.

They decide to make a graph to show their **difference** in growth. Look at the top of the page at the copy of their graph. First, they put the number of years (for their ages) along the bottom. Then they put the numbers (for their heights) in **centimeters** along the left-hand side.

Next, on each age line, the children mark a point exactly across from the number in centimeters that tells their height for that age. Then they draw a dashed line **connecting** each point that stands for Ricardo's growth, and they draw a solid line connecting all the points showing Julie's growth. When they **complete** their graph, they can easily see their heights at any age.

Both children were fifty centimeters at zero years (the day they were born). Can you see that Ricardo was 100 centimeters tall when he was five years old? To **determine** this, look along the bottom until you see five years old; then follow that line up until you meet Ricardo's (dashed) line. This line crosses or **intersects** the horizontal line at the one hundred centimeter mark.

Julie at five was not as tall as Ricardo. You can tell this because her (solid) line goes just below his. However, at ten years old Julie is taller than Ricardo. Just a **glance** at the graph shows you at what ages the two children were the same height.

A graph takes time and care to make, but once it is finished it helps answer many questions easily and quickly. It helps us to see facts.

THINKING IT OVER

(1) When were Ricardo and Julie the same height? _____

(2) Who was taller when both were nine? _____

(3) How tall was Julie when she was two years old?_____

STUDYING THE PASSAGE

(1) Find the Main Idea: Choose one.
    (a) How Ricardo and Julie keep a graph of their growth each year.
    (b) How Ricardo and Julie make a graph to compare their growth.
    (c) How easy it is to make a graph.
    (d) Why you should keep track of your growth. ____

(2) Find the Facts: Mark each one *true* or *false*.
    (a) Ricardo is measured every year by his mother. (a) ____
    (b) Ricardo and Julie are twelve years old. (b) ____
    (c) The number of years is on the bottom of the graph. (c) ____
    (d) Ricardo was one hundred centimeters tall when he was five years old. (d) ____

    (e)   Ricardo and Julie have already been measured by the
        school nurse.   (e) ____

    (f)   Ricardo and Julie were sitting on Ricardo's steps.   (f) ____

(3) Find the Order: Number the following in the order in which they appear in the
      passage.

    (a)   Ricardo and Julie are talking.   ____

    (b)   Julie is measured by her father.   ____

    (c)   Julie and Ricardo decide to make a graph.   ____

    (d)   Ricardo and Julie are sitting together.   ____

    (e)   A graph helps us see facts.   ____

(4) Go beyond the Facts: If Ricardo and Julie wanted to compare their growth with
      that of their friend, Toshiyuki, what *one* thing would they most likely do?

    (a)   Make three graphs.

    (b)   Add another line for Toshiyuki to their graph.

    (c)   They couldn't do it.

    (d)   Make a separate graph for Toshiyuki.   ____

USING THE WORDS

(1) Words and Their Meanings: Write the letter of the correct definition beside the
      word.

    ____ graph   (a) a quick look

    ____ annually   (b) a measurement of length that is equal to about 0.39 inch

    ____ difference   (c) to fasten or hook one thing to another

    ____ centimeter   (d) to figure out, to think through

    ____ to connect   (e) the way two or more things are not alike or not similar

    ____ to complete   (f) a chart that gives facts and information by carefully

    ____ to determine   placing lines and dots in certain places

    ____ to intersect   (g) to cross

    ____ glance   (h) every year

                              (i) to finish

(2) Write a paragraph using 2 of the vocabulary words. Use a separate piece of
      paper.

WRITING ABOUT IT Use a separate piece of paper for your answers.

(1) Make a graph showing the differences in growth between Olga and Kim. Mark Olga's heights in one color and Kim's heights in a different color.

At birth Olga was 13 in. (35 cm) Kim was 14 in. ($35\frac{1}{2}$ cm)
At age 2 Olga was $19\frac{1}{2}$ in. (49 cm) Kim was 20 in. ($50\frac{1}{2}$ cm)
At age 5 Olga was $42\frac{1}{2}$ in. (108 cm) Kim was 43 in. (109 cm)
At age 8 Olga was $49\frac{1}{2}$ in. (125 cm) Kim was 50 in. (127 cm)
At age 10 Olga was $54\frac{1}{2}$ in. (137 cm) Kim was $54\frac{1}{2}$ in. (137 cm)

(a) Who was the tallest at the age of 5?
(b) Who was the tallest at the age of 8?
(c) When were Olga and Kim the same height?

(2) You can show differences between people with a graph. But you can show more differences and give more details if you use words. Choose two classmates or members of your family and describe how they are different.

HOW HAWAII WAS CREATED

ABOUT THE PASSAGE

The Hawaiians have a myth explaining the **origin** of their islands. Where do you think they came from?

(a) the tears of a whale   (c) a hurricane

(b) out of the sea   (d) none of these

REASON FOR READING

To see how a common, everyday experience can be used to tell a magical story.

READ THE PASSAGE

Maui sat on the beach looking out to sea. He was waiting for his brothers to return from fishing. He had wanted to go fishing with them, but they said, "Why should we take you? We do all the work paddling, and you pull in all the fish." Maui had to admit this was true. He was just a little lazy.

To pass the time, Maui **fashioned** a fishhook from bone. He was a good carver, and soon it was ready for use. He held it up in the sunlight to admire it, and as he did so, he prayed to the gods to give it special powers.

At last Maui's brothers returned. "How many fish did you catch?" Maui asked.

"None," they answered. "There were no fish in the sea. There was nothing to catch but seaweed."

"You should have taken me," Maui told them.

"How do you think you can catch fish that aren't there?" his brothers asked crossly.

"Take me tomorrow and I will show you," said Maui with a **mischievous** grin.

The next day the brothers took Maui fishing with them. It was not because they believed he would catch any fish. Quite the opposite. They wanted to teach him a lesson for **boasting.**

When they were far out to sea, the brothers began to fish. But Maui lay back in the canoe, enjoying the sun.

"Why aren't you fishing?" the brothers asked Maui. "You said you could catch some fish, so why don't you start?"

"We're not far enough out," replied Maui, "paddle some more."

The brothers paddled farther out to sea. But Maui told them to go still further. They paddled so far that their island appeared as a **silhouette** on the horizon.

Finally, Maui said, "You can stop now."

Maui cast his line into the ocean and told his brothers, "Turn the canoe around and paddle back home. When you know I have caught a fish, paddle as strongly as you can, and don't look back. Remember, you must not look back."

The brothers **headed** for home. Soon there was a great tugging, and they knew Maui had caught a fish. The tugging increased, and they had to pull on the paddles with all their strength while Maui struggled with the fish.

"Paddle, paddle. Don't look back," Maui cried as he pulled with all his **might.**

"What kind of fish has Maui caught?" the brothers asked each other. "What fish can pull this strongly?"

Filled with curiosity, one brother looked back. "Wow!" he exclaimed, "Maui has caught land. He is **pulling up** islands!"

The brothers stopped and stared in amazement.

But Maui was furious. "Look what you have done," he shouted. "I was going to pull up a great land, but because you stopped and looked, I have only these islands!"

And that, so the story says, is how the Hawaiian islands, our fiftieth state, came to be.

THINKING ABOUT IT

(1) Where does the myth say Hawaii came from? _____

(2) Why was Maui disappointed? _____

_____

STUDYING THE PASSAGE

(1) Find the Main Idea: Choose one.
   (a) Why the brothers did not like taking Maui fishing.
   (b) How the brothers always did the work.
   (c) Why Hawaii is a good place to go fishing.
   (d) How a boy fished Hawaii out of the sea. ____

(2) Find the Facts: Mark each one *true* or *false*.

(a) The brothers did not want to take Maui fishing because he never helped. _____

(b) Maui made a fishing net. _____

(c) Maui would not fish until they were far out to sea. _____

(d) Maui told the brothers to stop paddling when he caught a fish. _____

(e) The brothers did not turn to see what Maui had caught. _____

(f) Maui was angry because the brothers stopped paddling. _____

(3) Find the Order: Number the following in the order in which they appear in the passage.

(a) Finally, Maui said, "You can stop now." _____

(b) "You should have taken me," Maui told them. _____

(c) The brothers stopped and stared. _____

(d) "Why aren't you fishing?" the brothers asked. _____

(e) To pass the time, Maui fashioned a fishhook. _____

(f) But Maui was furious. _____

(4) Go beyond the Facts: Which did you *not* learn from the story?

(a) Hawaii is made up of several islands.

(b) Hawaii was the last state to become part of America.

(c) Hawaii is made of rock from a volcano.

(d) Hawaii may have been different if the boys had continued paddling. _____

USING THE WORDS

(1) Words and Their Meanings: Write the letter of the correct definition beside the word.

_____ origin   (a) strength

_____ to fashion   (b) beginning; how something started

_____ mischievous   (c) to move or advance in a certain direction

_____ to boast   (d) to brag, to talk with too much pride and pleasure

_____ silhouette   (e) to make, form, or shape

_____ to head   (f) an outline; any dark shape seen against a light background

_____ might

_____ pulling up   (g) extracting

    (h) playful, sometimes tricky

(2) Write a paragraph using 2 of the words. Use a separate piece of paper.

WRITING ABOUT IT   Use a separate piece of paper for your answers.

(1) Find out the real origin of Hawaii. Then write an account of it.

(2) This myth tells about the origin of Hawaii. Make up a myth that tells about the origin of your state. It may help to find out your state flower, flag, or symbol.

THE BIBLE'S CREATION STORY*

ABOUT THE PASSAGE

The first book in the Bible is called "Genesis," which means "beginning" or "birth." It tells one of the oldest stories of the creation of the world. How many days did it take God to make the world?

REASON FOR READING

To notice the way words are repeated over and over and to see how this gives the writing a **rhythm** rather like poetry.

READ THE PASSAGE

In the beginning God created heaven and earth. And the earth was without **form,** and darkness was on the face of the deep. And the Spirit of God moved upon the face of the waters.

And God said, "Let there be light," and there was light. And he divided the light from the darkness. And he called the light Day, and the darkness he called Night. This was the first day.

On the second day, God said, "Let there be a **firmament** in the midst of the waters." And he made the firmament and divided the waters. And he called the firmament Heaven.

On the third day, God said, "Let the waters under heaven be gathered together into one place, and let the dry land appear." And he called the dry land Earth, and the waters he called Seas.

And God said, "Let the earth bring forth grass and trees, each bearing seed and fruit **after its own kind.**" And it was so.

When the fourth day came, God said, "Let there be lights in the firmament of the Heaven to divide the day from the night, and let them be for signs, and for seasons, and for days, and for years." Thus he made the sun, the moon, and the stars and set them in the firmament.

On the fifth day, God said, "Let the waters **bring forth** the moving **creatures** that have life, and **fowl** that may fly above the earth in the open firmament of heaven." Thus God created fish and fowl.

On the sixth day, God said, "Let the earth bring forth the living creatures, cattle and creeping things." Thus he created the animals.

*Adapted from Genesis 1:1–31.

And God said, "Let us make man." And he formed a man from the dust of the ground and breathed into his **nostrils** the breath of life.

When God finished, he saw that everything he had made was good. And on the seventh day, God rested. And he blessed the seventh day as a day of rest.

THINKING IT OVER

(1) How many days did it take God to make the world?_____

(2) What did God leave out when he made the world? _____

(3) On which day did God create the first creatures?_____

STUDYING THE PASSAGE

(1) Find the Main Idea: Choose one.
    (a) Why we have heaven and earth.
    (b) How the world was created.
    (c) How God created the first person.
    (d) How God rested on the seventh day.   _____

(2) Find the Facts: Mark each one *true* or *false*.
    (a) Before God started to labor, nothing had any shape.   (a) _____
    (b) God first made the earth.   (b) _____
    (c) God made the sky before he made the trees.   (c) _____
    (d) God put the sun and moon in the heavens to divide the day from night.   (d) _____
    (e) The first living things came out of the water.   (e) _____
    (f) God made the world in seven days.   (f) _____

(3) Find the Order: Number the following in the order in which they appear in the passage.
    (a) God said, "Let the dry land appear."   _____
    (b) Let the waters bring forth moving creatures.   _____
    (c) God said, "Let there be light."   _____
    (d) Let there be lights in Heaven to divide the day from night.   _____
    (e) On the seventh day, God rested.   _____

(4) Go beyond the Facts: Which one of the following is *not* true?

(a) The Bible tells how the world was created.

(b) The Bible is one of the oldest books in the world.

(c) The Bible's creation story is believed by everyone.

(d) The writing in the Bible is like poetry because it repeats words and has rhythm. _____

USING THE WORDS

(1) Words and Their Meanings: Write the letter of the correct definition beside the word.

____ rhythm	(a)	shape and size of something
____ form	(b)	living, moving things
____ firmament	(c)	sky; outer space
____ after its own kind	(d)	openings in the nose
____ to bring forth	(e)	of its own type
____ creatures	(f)	birds
____ fowl	(g)	to give out; to produce
____ nostrils	(h)	a flow of rising and falling sounds

(2) Write a paragraph using 2 of the vocabulary words. Use a separate piece of paper.

WRITING ABOUT IT   Use a separate piece of paper for your answers.

(1) A summary is a shortened form of a passage or a story. Reread the passage; then write a summary of how God made the world.

(2) Have fun with words. Describe the four seasons (spring, summer, fall, and winter) repeating words, so your writing has a rhythm like the passage.

HOW SOME NATIVE AMERICANS SAY PEOPLE WERE MADE

ABOUT THE PASSAGE

A long time ago, some Native Americans thought the coyote was the smartest of all the animals. They had many stories about coyote that showed her cleverness.

REASON FOR READING

To discover a lesson or deeper meaning in this story.

READ THE PASSAGE

The Coyote smiled and gave a little laugh. She had finished making the world and all the animals. She had only one thing left to do. She must make human beings.

She called the animals together. They sat around her in a circle.

"Now!" said Coyote. "I am going to make people. I would like your **advice.** Human beings must be the best of all the animals. What do you think such a creature should be like?"

The Cougar was the first to speak. "People must be able to roar like me," he said.

"Human beings must have **broad** tails to swim like me," said Beaver.

"And long legs to run fast," said Deer.

"They will be of no use without **keen** eyesight and wings," said the Owl.

They all began to talk at once. Each was sure that his or her idea was the best.

"Okay! Okay!" shouted Coyote. "Each of you may be right, but we can tell only by trying. Each animal must take a handful of wet earth and make a human being."

The animals each picked up a lump of dirt and started **molding** it. But Owl's came out looking like Owl, and Cougar's looked like Cougar. The Deer couldn't get the **antlers** right. Beaver soon gave up trying.

They were still messing about when the darkness came. Finally, they gave up and went to sleep.

Only Coyote did not sleep. She worked hard on her lump of dirt. After watching the other animals, she **combined** their ideas; she understood that human beings should have many different **qualities.** She realized, too, that humans must be different from the animals.

When the morning came, Coyote's work was finished. She had made a man and a woman.

THINKING IT OVER

(1) Why did some people think the coyote was the smartest animal? _____

_____

(2) Why didn't the other animals manage to do what the coyote did? _____

_____

STUDYING THE PASSAGE

(1) Find the Main Idea: Choose one.
    (a) How the animals made the first people.
    (b) How human beings were made from dirt.
    (c) How a coyote made the first man and woman.
    (d) What to do when you cannot get to sleep. ____

(2) Find the Facts: Mark each one _true_ or _false_.
    (a) Coyote asked the animals to help her. (a) ____
    (b) Cougar wanted the first person to have a loud voice. (b) ____
    (c) Owl did not want people to be able to fly. (c) ____
    (d) Each animal thought he or she had the best idea. (d) ____
    (e) The beaver's creation was the most like a human being. (e) ____
    (f) Coyote slept while the others worked. (f) ____

(3) Find the Order: Number the following in the order in which they appear in the passage.
    (a) Each animal picked up a handful of dirt. ____
    (b) Owl said, "They will be of no use without wings." ____
    (c) Cougar spoke first. ____
    (d) Coyote called the animals together. ____
    (e) Coyote realized human beings should have different qualities. ____

(4) Go beyond the Facts: What _two_ ideas or deeper meanings can you find in the story?
    (a) You can learn a lot by listening.
    (b) If you talk loud enough, you will make yourself heard.
    (c) It is better to act than to talk.
    (d) Many hands are better than one. ____ ____

USING THE WORDS

(1) Words and Their Meanings: Write the letter of the correct definition beside the
     word. One word has *two* meanings.

     ____ advice   (a) telling another the right thing to do
     ____ broad   (b) sharp or quick in seeing, hearing, thinking, etc.
     ____ keen   (c) to make into a shape; to form
     ____ qualities   (d) horns of a deer
     ____ antlers   (e) wide, not narrow
     ____ to combine   (f) tiny living growth on spoiled food
     ____ mold   (g) to mix or put together as one
     ____   (h) features that make something what it is;
                                characteristics

(2) Write a paragraph using 2 of the words. Use a separate piece of paper.

WRITING ABOUT IT   Use a separate piece of paper for your answers.

(1) What do you think the other animals thought of the Coyote's man and woman?
     Tell what happened when they woke up and what they said to Coyote.

(2) Who do you think is the smartest animal? Write a story about it.

A DIFFERENT KIND OF HOME

ABOUT THE PASSAGE

The bedroom in this story belongs to David Copperfield, the hero of *David Copperfield*, by Charles Dickens. David's room is in an unusual place. Where do you think it is?

REASON FOR READING

To notice how the writer helps you see the room by giving a lot of details. And to understand that a descriptive passage does not have to be long if the words are well chosen.

READ THE PASSAGE

It was the most **complete** and most **desirable** bedroom ever seen. It was in the **stern** of the **vessel.** There was a little window where the **rudder** used to go through, and a little looking glass, just the right height for me, nailed against the wall. The looking glass was **framed** with oyster shells. There was also a little bed with just room enough to get into, and a **nosegay** of seaweed in the blue mug on the table. The walls were whitewashed as white as milk, and the **patchwork bedspread** made my eyes **ache** with its brightness.

THINKING IT OVER

(1) Where is this bedroom? _____

(2) List three words that helped you to guess. _____

_____

STUDYING THE PASSAGE

(1) Find the Main Idea: Choose one.

    (a) Everything was small in the bedroom.

    (b) The room was a bedroom.

    (c) It was a perfect bedroom.

    (d) It was a strange bedroom.   ____

(2) Find the Facts: Mark each one *true* or *false*.

    (a) The bedroom seemed to have everything David wanted.   (a) ____

    (b) There were oyster shells around the window.   (b) ____

    (c) The looking glass was just the right height.   (c) ____

    (d) The mug was red.   (d) ____

    (e) The walls of the bedroom were blue.   (e) ____

    (f) The patchwork bedspread was very bright.   (f) ____

(3) Find the Order: Number the following in the order in which they appear in the passage.

    (a) There was a little window.   (a) ____

    (b) It was the most complete and most desirable bedroom ever seen.   (b) ____

    (c) There was a patchwork bedspread.   (c) ____

    (d) A looking glass was nailed to the wall.   (d) ____

    (e) A mug was on the table.   (e) ____

(4) Go beyond the Facts: What is the writer telling you in his description of the room? Which answer could *not* be correct?

    (a) Everything but the bed was just perfect for David Copperfield.

    (b) The home was in the water.

    (c) There was not much space in the room.

    (d) The person describing the room was probably young.   ____

USING THE WORDS

(1) Words and Their Meanings: Write the letter of the correct definition beside the word. One word has *two* meanings.

____ complete	(a)	a bedcover made from cloth of many colors and shapes
____ desirable		
____ stern	(b)	strict
____	(c)	to hurt, to feel pain
____ vessel	(d)	worth having; attractive
____ rudder	(e)	back end of a boat
____ framed	(f)	having everything; whole
____ nosegay	(g)	enclosed with a border (like a picture)
____ patchwork bedspread	(h)	a bunch of flowers
____ to ache	(i)	part of the boat used to steer
	(j)	a boat

(2) Write a paragraph using 2 of the vocabulary words.

WRITING ABOUT IT   Use a separate piece of paper for your answers.

(1) Imagine you were the person to sleep in the room described in the passage. Write a letter to a friend describing what your first night was like.

(2) Describe what you think would be a perfect bedroom. Remember to pay special attention to your choice of words.

ANOTHER CREATION STORY

ABOUT THE PASSAGE

In this Native American legend, a rabbit, the king of the animals, is able to create the earth with the help of a tough and courageous muskrat.

REASON FOR READING

To watch how the **character** of Muskrat is different from what she seems to be at first.

READ THE PASSAGE

In the beginning the earth was covered by deep, deep water. On this water **floated** a **raft,** and on the raft were all the animals. One of the cleverest of all the animals was Michabo, the Great Rabbit.

The animals were very tired of living on the small raft. They wished they had some land with green grass growing on it. They asked the Rabbit to make some land.

Michabo thought for a while, and then he sent the beaver into the water.

"Bring back some land, Beaver," said Rabbit.

But Beaver could not find any land.

So Rabbit sent the Sea Otter in search of land. Sea Otter dived deep, but he could not find any land either, and he soon returned **exhausted.**

The animals were in **despair,** when Muskrat spoke.

"I will go," she said.

The animals laughed.

"You are too small and weak," they cried.

But Muskrat dived into the water.

Two days went by and Muskrat did not return. The animals said to each other, "We knew she couldn't do it!"

On the evening of the third day, Beaver **spotted** something swimming toward them. **Hastily,** they began to row the raft to meet the swimmer. It was Muskrat!

Rabbit said, "We thought you were dead!" But Muskrat was not dead. In her paws she was holding a tiny speck of dirt. She handed it to Rabbit, and from it he made the world.

THINKING IT OVER

(1) From what was the world made? _____

_____

(2) Who found it? _____

_____

(3) What is a legend? _____

_____

STUDYING THE PASSAGE

(1) Find the Main Idea: Choose one.
    (a) An unusual sea trip.
    (b) What happens when some animals go for a sea trip.
    (c) How Muskrat showed she was not weak.
    (d) How the world was created by some animals.   _____

(2) Find the Facts: Mark each one *true* or *false*.
    (a) All the animals were unhappy on the raft.   (a) _____
    (b) They were near dry land.   (b) _____
    (c) Three animals tried to find earth.   (c) _____
    (d) The animals told Muskrat that she was small and weak. (d) _____
    (e) Muskrat was dead.   (e) _____
    (d) Muskrat brought back a speck of dirt.   (f) _____

(3) Find the Order: Number the following in the order in which they appear in the
    passage.
    (a) They asked Rabbit to make some land.   _____
    (b) Sea Otter dived deep.   _____
    (c) On the water floated a raft.   _____
    (d) Muskrat was holding a speck of dirt.   _____
    (e) On the evening of the third day, they saw Muskrat.   _____

(4) Go beyond the Facts: According to this legend, which *one* of the following is true?

    (a) The other animals had good reasons for doubting Muskrat.

    (b) Even a quiet and small creature may do a great and difficult action.

    (c) Usually our first opinions or ideas about others are correct.

    (d) If others have tried to do something and have failed, it's best to give up trying to do it.   ____

USING THE WORDS

(1) Words and Their Meanings: Write the letter of the correct definition beside the word. One word has *two* meanings.

____ character	(a) very, very tired
____ to float	(b) a flat boat with no sides
____ raft	(c) all the qualities that make a person different
____ exhausted	from others
____ despair	(d) covered with little dots
____ spotted	(e) quickly
____	(f) caught sight of
____ hastily	(g) without hope
	(h) to lie on the water without sinking

(2) Write a paragraph using 2 of the vocabulary words. Use a separate piece of paper.

WRITING ABOUT IT   Use a separate piece of paper for your answers.

(1) Read a legend of your choice. Then write the story in your own words.

(2) In this book you have read different stories about how the world and people were created. Make up your own story explaining how the world or people were created.

THE ART OF CREATING CARTOONS

Thank heavens! Tourists at last!

ABOUT THE PASSAGE

What do you think of this picture?

(a) It's funny.

(b) It's silly.

(c) It's clever.

REASON FOR READING

This passage is short to give you practice in speeding up your reading. Read it as fast as you can; then see if you can give the four uses of cartoons.

READ THE PASSAGE

Did you laugh at the picture at the top of the page? The artist hopes that you did because that is what he was trying to do. He is a cartoonist, and the pictures he makes are called cartoons.

Cartoons are usually funny. They are also easy to read and understand. But cartoons are not easy to create. First, cartoonists have to be able to draw. Second, they have to think a lot to come up with good ideas. Third, they have to be able to put these ideas in **visual** form, so they can be seen and understood in a glance.

Some cartoonists make things bigger, or **exaggerate** them, in their drawings to make you notice them. This is seen especially in caricatures.

Caricatures are pictures of people that show parts of them larger than they really are to draw your attention to them. What parts do you notice in this caricature?

Caricatures have been used for **centuries** to **mock** or make fun of well known people, and they are still used today.

But cartoons are not always meant to be funny. They are also used to tell stories, such as the comic strips in the newspaper. Comic strips are made up of a series of drawings which are read in a **sequence.** The story is told mainly through the pictures, although words are often included. Some **famous** ones are *Peanuts, Doonesbury, Garfield,* and *Spiderman*. Which is your favorite?

Long vowels say their own names.

Cartoons can also be used to **inform** people about something. They are used in all sorts of ways from advertisements selling toothpaste to teaching aids in a spelling class like the cartoon to the left.

The most difficult cartoons to make are **animated** cartoons. These are the ones you see on television and at the movies. The animals and people look real in these cartoons because they move and talk. To find out more about these, read the next selection.

THINKING IT OVER

(1) What do you call someone who creates cartoons? _____

(2) What is a caricature? _____

_____

(3) What is an animated cartoon? _____

_____

STUDYING THE PASSAGE

(1) Find the Main Idea: Choose one.
    (a) How to make a cartoon.
    (b) How to read a cartoon.
    (c) Facts about cartoons.
    (d) A caricature is a cartoon.   ____

(2) Find the Facts: Mark each one *true* or *false*.
   (a) Cartoons are simple to read but difficult to create.   (a) ____
   (b) A cartoon must be easy to read.   (b) ____
   (c) The caricature in the passage makes the man's nose and chin
       seem bigger than they really are.   (c) ____
   (d) Cartoons are always funny.   (d) ____
   (e) The spelling cartoon teaches long-vowel sounds in a lighthearted
       way.   (e) ____
   (f) Cartoons can actually be made to seem lifelike.   (f) ____

(3) Find the Order: Number the following in the order in which they appear in the
    passage.
   (a) Some cartoons make things bigger or exaggerate them.   ____
   (b) He is a cartoonist.   ____
   (c) Cartoons are not always meant to be funny.   ____
   (d) These are the ones you can see on television and at the movies. ____
   (e) A cartoonist must be able to draw.   ____

(4) Go beyond the Facts: Which *one* is right?
   (a) Cartoons take a long time to read.
   (b) Cartoons are drawings that make everything seem bigger than it really is.
   (c) The best cartoons are always funny.
   (d) The best cartoons are easy to understand.   ____

USING THE WORDS

(1) Words and Their Meanings: Write the letter of the correct definition beside the
    word.

   ____ visual   (a) to make something seem greater than it really is
   ____ to exaggerate   (b) to make fun of
   ____ century   (c) well known
   ____ to mock   (d) one hundred years
   ____ sequence   (e) to tell; to let someone know
   ____ famous   (f) that can be seen
   ____ to inform   (g) moving and talking as though alive
   ____ animated   (h) the following of one thing after another

(2) Write a paragraph using 2 of the vocabulary words.

WRITING ABOUT IT   Use a separate piece of paper for your answers.

(1) Describe the four uses of cartoons, giving examples of each one.

(2) Have fun. Create your own cartoon.

Selection 31—Subject: The Arts
Theme: Personalities in the Arts

A MAN WITH A DREAM

ABOUT THE PASSAGE

One cartoonist, Walt Disney, was not **satisfied** with making **sketches** and drawings on paper. He wanted to make his drawings move and talk. This passage tells how he invented animated cartoons.

REASON FOR READING

To learn about one person who worked hard to make his idea succeed.

READ THE PASSAGE

On March 25, 1969, the President of the United States, Richard Nixon, **honored** the memory of a famous man. This man was not a hero. He was a simple man who loved children. His name was Walt Disney. He spent his life dreaming dreams and making them come true. One of these dreams was Mickey Mouse; another was Snow White and the Seven Dwarfs.

Walt Disney was not satisfied just to draw pictures; his biggest dream was to see these pictures move and hear them speak. So he invented animated cartoons. His drawings appeared to have a life of their own. Once he had discovered how to make his pictures move, he wanted them to speak as well, but it was a long time before this was possible.

To animate the cartoons took years of hard work. At first the films were short. This was because it took so long to make the hundreds of drawings needed for each one. Every **movement** each character made had to be drawn separately and photographed with a special camera. Walt almost gave up the whole idea. Finally he used a team of artists called **animators;** then work moved much more quickly. Now the process is done with computers.

Walt Disney's first production was a series of short films called the *Alice Comedies.* For these, a live girl was teamed with the cartoon characters. His early films were so successful that he formed a company of his own. Mickey Mouse was born in 1928 in Disney's first sound film.

One after another the characters Walt created left his drawing board to please audiences all over the world. Some of Disney's best films, however, were not animated. They were about nature. *The Living Desert* and *The*

Vanishing *Prairie* took months of patient work on the part of the camera **operators.**

Although the man who loved children has gone, his dream children are very much alive. People still enjoy watching Mickey and Minnie Mouse and Daisy and Donald Duck.

THINKING IT OVER

(1) What was Walt Disney's dream? _____

_____

(2) What is the name for the art Walt Disney invented?_____

_____

STUDYING THE PASSAGE

Find the Main Idea: Choose one.
   (a) The story of a clever man.
   (b) How a man made his dream come true.
   (c) How to make cartoons come alive.
   (d) How to make a movie.   _____

(2) Find the Facts: Mark each one *true* or *false*.
   (a) Walt Disney loved children.   (a) ____
   (b) Walt Disney created *Peanuts*.   (b) ____
   (c) Mickey Mouse was born in 1928.   (c) ____
   (d) Every movement had to be drawn separately.   (d) ____
   (e) A team of artists created each animated cartoon.   (e) ____
   (f) President Kennedy honored Disney.   (f) ____

(3) Find the Order: Number the following in the order in which they appear in the passage.
   (a) A live girl was teamed with the cartoon characters.   _____
   (b) He invented "animated cartoons."   _____
   (c) One of these dreams was Mickey Mouse.   _____
   (d) Nowadays the process is done with computers.   _____
   (e) Some of the best films are those about nature.   _____

(4) Go beyond the Facts: Which *one* was Walt Disney's dream?

    (a) To make a lot of money.

    (b) To make children happy.

    (c) To make his characters come alive.

    (d) To become famous.   ____

USING THE WORDS

(1) Words and Their Meanings: Write the letter of the correct definition beside the word.

____	satisfied	(a)	a person who runs a machine
____	sketch	(b)	disappearing
____	to honor	(c)	changes in position
____	movements	(d)	a quick drawing
____	animators	(e)	artists who make animated cartoons
____	vanishing	(f)	pleased
____	operator	(g)	to have respect for

(2) Write a paragraph using 2 of the vocabulary words.

WRITING ABOUT IT   Use a separate piece of paper for your answers.

(1) Pretend you have to give someone a test on this selection. Make up 6 questions that you think would check whether he or she has taken in all the facts.

(2) Walt Disney had a dream. Write about one of your dreams. If you don't have a dream, make one up.